FAUST THE THEOLOGIAN

Jaroslav Pelikan

Faust the Theologian

Yale University Press

New Haven and London

Designed by James J. Johnson. Set in Walbaum Roman type by The Composing Room of Michigan, Inc. Printed in the United States of America by Vail-Ballou Press, Binghamton, New York.

Library of Congress Cataloging-in-Publication Data

Pelikan, Jaroslav Jan, 1923–

    Faust the theologian / Jaroslav Pelikan.

      p.   cm.

    Includes bibliographical references.

    ISBN 0-300-06288-5 (cloth: alk. paper)

        0-300-07064-0 (pbk.: alk. paper)

    1. Goethe, Johann Wolfgang von, 1749–1832. Faust.   2. Goethe, Johann Wolfgang von, 1749–1832—Religion.   I. Title.

PT1925.P36   1995

832'.6—dc20   94-37989

                                                            CIP

A catalogue record for this book is available from the British Library.

The paper in this book meets the guidelines for permanence and durability of the Committee on Production Guidelines for Book Longevity of the Council on Library Resources.

10   9   8   7   6   5   4   3   2

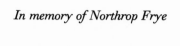

In memory of Northrop Frye

Contents

Preface

ALTHOUGH I HAVE BEEN READING Goethe's *Faust* every year since I was in secondary school and through such reading have committed large chunks of its German to memory, I have always had a certain diffidence about infiltrating the formidable ranks of the Goethe specialists by trying to make it the subject of a book. What finally began to overcome that diffidence was the publication in 1990 of a little book that I dedicated to the memory of my beloved friend, A. Bartlett Giamatti, *Eternal Feminines: Three Theological Allegories in Dante's "Paradiso."* For although it was based on a close reading of the *Divine Comedy* that had also been going on for many (though fewer) years, I remained much more deeply steeped in Goethe's masterpiece than in Dante's, as the very title of the book on Dante indicates; and the generous reception accorded to that modest effort by the *Dantista* establishment emboldens me to hope that Goethe scholars may be equally hospitable to a historian of ideas, even of theological ideas. The invitation to deliver the Willson Lectures for 1993 at Southwestern University in Georgetown, Texas, provided me with the opportunity to begin putting my interpretation into final form.

Throughout this book I have accepted the readings, spelling, and punctuation of the texts of *Faust* and of *Urfaust* as these appear in Trunz 1968. Following the lead prescribed by Boyle 1991 in his preface, I have translated all the German, quoting only the more important poetic passages in German as well. These translations are basically my own and have aimed to be literal rather than literary; but I have gratefully consulted, and sometimes borrowed from, other English translations, discussed by Frantz 1949 and by Atkins in Mahal 1973, 219–26. Among such translations, Fairley 1970, which renders Goethe into English prose instead of trying to reproduce the sense in verse, is often (though certainly not always) more sensitive to the theological nuances; I have in most instances also followed Barker Fairley's way of Anglicizing the names of places, characters, and scenes. Because of its importance for my reading of such key passages in *Faust* as lines 1851–55, a special problem of translation has been the German word *Wissenschaft*. After trying various alternative renderings in successive drafts— "scholarship," "learning," and even "research"—I have returned to the conclusion that, despite its imprecision in popular usage today, I should use the English word *science* as it has long been employed, not only for "Naturwissenschaft" as natural science, the subject of chapter 2, but for each of the hundred fields (657) of "Wissenschaft" in which Doctor Faust was engaged. For the same reason I have decided, again despite the imprecision of popular usage, to call him "Doctor" in chapter 1 even when the specific branch of science under consideration is not medicine but "alas, theology, too."

It will be obvious that in what Bruford 1967, 2–3 calls "the argument between the 'Fragmentarier,' the first of whom was Kuno Fischer, and the many 'Unitarier'" among the interpreters of *Faust*, I am definitely a disciple of the latter group of scholars, because I pay primary attention to the work as a whole rather than to its individual components. In so doing I have benefited from the massive body of monographic literature—the most pertinent of which, much of it assembled in the invaluable Speck Collection at Yale, is listed in the Bibliography—and from the commentaries, among which (in alphabetical order) Arens 1982, Arens 1989, Boyle 1987, Buchwald 1964, Hamlin 1976, May 1936, and Trunz 1968

have been especially helpful to me. Even more immediately helpful have been my devoted editors, John G. Ryden and Laura Jones
Dooley, and my colleague and friend, Theodore Ziolkowski, whose
careful and critical reading of the manuscript provided me with
good ideas and rescued me from some bad ones.

The curator of the Speck Collection and of the entire German
Literature section of the Beinecke Rare Book and Manuscript Library at Yale, Christa Sammons, graciously assembled for my consideration a massive number of illustrations of *Faust* from those
holdings. Of these, the series of copper engravings executed by the
late Peter Lipman-Wulf immediately caught my eye, and the
portrait of Faust as philosopher and scientist struck me as so appropriate that it might almost have been done with my portrayal in
mind. I am grateful to Barbara Lipman-Wulf for her permission to
reproduce it on the jacket.

Over the years I have had the opportunity to discuss many of
these problems and passages with my late colleague Hermann J.
Weigand, who in the course of those discussions generously gave
me not only many individual insights but his own set of the *Fest-
ausgabe* of works of Goethe, with his marginalia scattered through
the volumes; it is from that edition that I am quoting works other
than *Faust*, for example, *Wilhelm Meister.*

The book is dedicated to the memory of my friend Northrop
Frye, with whom I received an honorary doctorate in 1976 and
from whom I then received one in 1989, for his gift of combining
literary scholarship and theological scholarship without confusing
them.

CHAPTER ONE

Faust as Doctor of Theology

AT LEAST FOUR MONUMENTAL DRAMAS in the spiritual and literary history of the West are situated in the framework of the days of Holy Week: Palm Sunday was, according to the custom in Leipzig, the day for the performance of Johann Sebastian Bach's *Passion of Our Lord According to Saint Matthew;*[1] the morning of Good Friday was the setting for the opening of Dante Alighieri's *Divine Comedy;*[2] that day is also, in the Good Friday Spell, the time of the climax, both dramatically and musically, of Richard Wagner's *Parsifal,* when "every creature gives thanks, everything that blooms and soon perishes, as today a Nature freed from sin reaches the day in which its innocence is restored";[3] and the night of Holy Saturday, with the choir of angels intoning, "Christ is risen!" (737), and the unbelieving scholar explaining, "I hear the message all right, but what I lack is the faith" (765), begins the action of Johann Wolfgang von Goethe's *Faust.*

1. Spitta 1951, 2:538; Pelikan 1986, 77–78.
2. "Temp'era dal principio del mattino, / e 'l sol montava 'n su con quelle stelle / ch'eran con lui quando l'amor divino / mosse di prima quelle cose belle." Dante, *Inferno,* I, 37–40.
3. "Das dankt dann alle Kreatur / Was all da blüht und bald erstirbt, / Da die entsündigte Natur / Heut ihren Unschuldstag erwirbt." Wagner, *Parsifal,* act III.

As the history of its reception over the past century and a half has demonstrated, it is possible to read Goethe's *Faust* in many ways.[4] Being a reworking, or rather a recasting, of a Faust legend that goes back to the Middle Ages or perhaps even earlier, it has led comparativists and historians of literature to continue to analyze its connections with that legend.[5] There is a long tradition of interpreters who have seen it as a vast allegory, or perhaps better a series of allegories, about the human condition in the modern age.[6] Because, as a recent biography of Goethe suggests, "more must be known, or at any rate there must be more to know, about Goethe than about almost any other human being"[7] on account of the massive amount of source material, it is almost inevitable that this, his most comprehensive work, should have become for many scholars a *roman à clef*, or an *autobiographie à clef*. Each incident, and sometimes it seems each phrase, finds a counterpart in that source material about his life and thought, above all in *Wilhelm Meister* and in the autobiographical *Dichtung und Wahrheit*—he did, after all, call his writings "fragments of a great confession." Early in the twentieth century, one of the most far-reaching interpretations of *Faust*, Oswald Spengler's *Decline of the West*, saw in the figure of Goethe's hero "the *Faustian* soul, whose prime-symbol is pure and limitless space. . . . Here infinite solitude is felt as the home of the Faustian soul."[8] Part One, at any rate, has easily lent itself to Marxist interpreters as a bourgeois tragedy about the exploitation of a proletarian Margarete by a member of the élite.[9] The relation between technology and society represented by

4. Klett 1939 is a fairly exhaustive collection of titles; M.-J. Fischer 1983 and R. Scholz 1983 are historical accounts of many of these ways of reading the work, especially in German scholarship; Mulloy 1944 considers an aspect of its reception that has special pertinence to this book; Ugrinsky 1987 is a collection of representative studies; and Williams 1987, 47–62, "The Reception of Goethe's Faust," is a convenient overall summary.

5. Palmer and More 1965 treat this aspect of the drama.

6. Brenn 1981 and especially Schlaffer 1981 are representative examples.

7. Boyle 1991, 1:vii.

8. Spengler 1983, 1:183, 186.

9. M.-J. Fischer 1983, 72–85, is a discussion of "Das frühe marxistische Goethe-Bild (Georg Lukács)." Class consciousness manifests itself already upon Margarete's first appearance, when she is surprised at being addressed by the designation "Fräulein," not appropriate to her social class (2605–8).

Faust's effort to tame the sea, late in Part Two, has raised for some readers, notably the distinguished physicist Werner Heisenberg, many of the problems of that relation played out on a dramatic scale.[10] Freudian readings of *Faust*—of the closing scene, for example[11]—have sought to relate it to various experiences of the poet's childhood and earlier life. To the disciples of Carl Jung, in contrast, *Faust* has provided a host of opportunities to penetrate the tale's symbolism in search of a deeper meaning.[12] The ideologues of National Socialism, and those literary scholars who became their willing followers, saw the drama as a glorification of the qualities of Aryan culture; conversely, the collapse of that ideology brought with it the deepening conviction that it would never be possible to read *Faust* in quite the same way again.[13] And it is not necessary to be a feminist to agree with the criticism that as a drama written by a poet who freely admitted that he found the charms of young women irresistible and who went on pursuing them when he was well into his seventies, *Faust* is also the account of a protagonist whose eventual fulfillment is made possible only by the immolation of two women—Gretchen the innocent, and then Helen the beautiful—and who is said to achieve eventual salvation through being drawn upward by the Eternal Feminine of the final line.

The reading of *Faust* in this book, without involving itself in an ongoing debate with any of these and other interpretations, is an effort to look at the character of Faust as, in one critic's delightful phrase, "an ungovernable theological problem-child,"[14] and thus to relate it to theology, theology as an account of religious faith but also theology as an academic discipline among other academic disciplines.[15] Despite the several nineteenth-century efforts to make him into one, Goethe was not an orthodox Christian theo-

10. Heisenberg 1967, 27–42.

11. Eissler 1963, 2:861–66.

12. See especially the comments of Emrich 1953, 38–67, but also his book of 1957.

13. Würtenberg 1949, written in the aftermath of that collapse, bears the significant subtitle: "Das Ende des faustischen Menschen."

14. E. Heller 1966, 28.

15. On this academic dimension of the work, Kroner 1957, 153–73, and Kluge 1982 are especially pertinent.

logian, nor did he want to be seen as one.[16] But he did want to be seen as standing, in some sense, within the Christian tradition—*and* within the Classical tradition *and* within the humanistic tradition *and* within the scientific tradition![17] A justification for taking this approach to *Faust* in relation to theology may also be found in the ever-deepening unawareness of the Christian tradition among Goethe's present-day readers, including sometimes even the scholarly ones. Their puzzled references (to remain for now only within Part One) to Margarete's church attendance at the beginning of the Gretchen tragedy (2621–6), or to her prayer before the Virgin Mary as Mater Dolorosa (3588–3619) and her attendance at a Requiem Mass with the singing of the *Dies irae* (3776–3834) near the end of it, often seem to treat these like the exotic rituals of some distant tribe, interesting and intelligible only to cultural anthropologists; Goethe, by contrast, regardless of what he may or may not have believed, knew and understood such things quite well.[18] The extent to which a theological reading of *Faust* constitutes a problem will be evident from a study of various of the books and articles listed in the Bibliography.[19] This is, then, not a book about Goethe's theology or theolog*ies*, whatever it or they may have been, but, as the book's title specifies, about Faust himself as theologian. For despite Goethe's frequently quoted words about "fragments of a great confession," both Goethe's beliefs and Faust's beliefs are too complicated for any simple identification of the one with the other. Readers of *Faust*, including scholarly ones, would be well advised to heed the recent warning that it is in the "closeness of relationship between the writer and the play, rather than between the writer

16. To list some nineteenth-century studies chronologically (further details in the Bibliography): Gantzer 1857; Beyschlag 1877; Durrani 1877; Bergedorf 1881; Rieger 1881; Kalthoff 1901. Twentieth-century discussions, which are in general far more circumspect, include: Obenauer 1921; Franz 1932; Schnitzer 1932; Weissleder 1936; Münzhuber 1947; Busch 1949; Meinhold 1958; Möbus 1964; Reimann 1967; Jarras 1969; Richter 1973; Schüpbach 1980; Thielicke 1982; Schöne 1987; Luke 1990. In a special category is Harnack 1923, 141–70.

17. See the summary of Bergstraesser 1949, 29–46, and the concluding remarks of Kohlschmidt 1955, 119.

18. See Cooledge 1932 for some interesting details.

19. For example, from a comparison between Thielicke 1982 and Luke 1990, with its sharp critique of Thielicke.

and the play's principal character, that the special status of *Faust* among Goethe's works is grounded."[20] Other works of his will come into consideration here chiefly as, in a broad sense, lexicographical resources for understanding the language of *Faust.* The book is, moreover, about Faust's theology in both of the senses of that term mentioned earlier, the religious and the academic.[21]

Heinrich Faust (the name Heinrich, the closing word of Part One [4612], was apparently one of Goethe's additions to the traditional Faust story, in which the man's name had been Johann)[22] is a man of great learning, especially if, despite the language of Mephistopheles about restoring his lost youth to him (2348–50), he is only thirty years old, as modern interpreters seems to have agreed.[23] He is, as the old peasant calls him, "a man of enormous erudition" (984). Employing no more sarcasm than usual, Mephistopheles also greets him that way when they first meet: "I salute the learned gentleman!" (1325). Later, Mephistopheles does seem to be speaking also for Faust, and for the entire community of learned men, when, wearing Faust's doctoral garb, he exclaims: "I know it well, to be far along in years and still a student, in fact an old mossback! Even a man of learning goes on studying because there is nothing else he can do. One builds a modest house of cards, but even the greatest mind never completes it" (6637–41).[24]

Although there seems to be no direct mention in *Faust* of a university or other institution of higher learning to whose faculty he belongs, in *Urfaust* Faust does refer to himself as a "professor" (7); also in *Urfaust,* Mephistopheles disguised as Faust speaks in a "professorial tone" (403). It would surely be forcing the interpretation to take the removal of those references in the definitive version

20. Boyle 1991, 1:632.

21. Henning 1970, 298–300, lists only some of the studies that have dealt with this theme.

22. See Hamlin 1976, 83–84 n. 2.

23. Resenhöfft 1973, 200–211.

24. Ich weiß es wohl, bejahrt und noch Student, / Bemooster Herr! Auch ein gelehrter Mann / Studiert so fort, weil er nicht anders kann. / So baut man sich ein mäßig Kartenhaus, / Der größte Geist baut's doch nicht völlig aus.

as implying that for that version he is no longer a professor; for he continues to have students, whom he has been "leading by the nose, back and forth, for the past ten years" (361–63). New students, moreover, come to him for advice about how to become as learned as he is, and in as many fields; as one says, "I would like to become really learned and to comprehend everything in Earth and Heaven, all of science and all of Nature" (1898–1901).[25] Those two terms, "all of science and all of Nature," cover the spectrum of scholarship and science, as do the words "everything in Earth and Heaven." Surrounded by his library, Faust speaks of himself as "hemmed in all the way to the lofty ceiling by this stack of books—worm-eaten and dust-covered, with sooty paper stuck over them" (402–5). And in that setting he asks, "Should I perhaps read in a thousand books?" (661). Those thousands of books, moreover, come "out of a hundred scholarly disciplines" (657).

In at least some of these scholarly disciplines Faust has taken advanced university degrees. On their visit to the Witch's Kitchen, Mephistopheles introduces Faust to one witch as "a man who holds many degrees" (2581), and Faust says of himself at the beginning of the drama: "I carry the title of Master, and even of Doctor" (360). It is as "Doctor" that he is known throughout Part One. That form of reference and address seems to be a customary way for the common people to speak about a scholar, for it is also as "Doctor Luther" that the German Reformer is identified in the tavern song that Brander, one of the Merry Companions, sings in Auerbach's Cellar in Leipzig (2129). "Herr Doktor" is used as a term of authentic, if fawning, respect when it comes from Wagner, Faust's *famulus*, or academic assistant (941), or from the old peasant (981). It is a considerably more mocking title when Mephistopheles uses it (in conjunction with the polite third-person plural form of address in the verb) in speaking about Margarete's interrogation of Faust concerning his religious faith (or lack of it), "I followed it very closely: the Doctor was being catechized" (3522–23),[26] or about

25. Ich wünschte recht gelehrt zu werden, / Und möchte gern, was auf der Erden / Und in dem Himmel ist, erfassen, / Die Wissenschaft und die Natur.
26. Ich hab's ausführlich wohl vernommen, / Herr Doktor wurden da katechisiert.

Valentin's attack on him (3704). Mephistopheles calls Faust "Doctor" even on Walpurgis Night while he is running interference for him through the "mob" (4024). Yet the title seems to be employed only rarely for Faust in Part Two (cf. 6663), for reasons that are not obvious. Perhaps it is that, beginning already with the pact and then especially with the death of Gretchen, Faust is seen as having put behind him the entire apparatus and nomenclature of the dry-as-dust scholar. The academic titles that do appear in Part Two, including "Doctor," are applied to others rather than to Faust himself, as when Wagner, the sometime academic assistant, is identified ironically as Faust's unlikely successor, "the distinguished Doctor Wagner, who now holds first place in the world of learning" (6643–44), or when Mephistopheles disguises himself as a docent (6588), or when, in that disguise, he has an interview with the Bachelor of Arts (6689–6806), whom he had met earlier as a prospective student (1868–2048).

But if Faust can say, "I carry the title of Master, and even of Doctor" (360), it does not seem out of place to ask him, following the form of inquiry in which Mephistopheles puts the question in his discussion with the student, "You must declare yourself: Which faculty do you choose?" (1896–97). And again a bit later Mephistopheles asks: "But make your choice of a faculty!" (1968). Among the "hundred scholarly disciplines" (657) represented in his library, then, which are the ones of which Doctor Faust is a "Master" or a "Doctor," and which "faculty" (or faculties) had he himself selected when he was only a student? His own opening sigh, "With strain and sweat I have studied my way all through philosophy, jurisprudence, and medicine—and, alas, theology, too" (354–57),[27] is a list not of scholarly disciplines but of entire faculties, all four of the faculties at the German university (in Goethe's day, if not in Faust's). In his claims to have "studied his way all through" the curriculum of each, he does not specify whether this represents the chronological order in which he has studied them, with theology coming last, or whether this is a traditional arrangement; in either event it could be taken as an ironic acknowledgment of

27. Habe nun, ach! Philosophie, / Juristerei und Medizin, / Und leider auch Theologie / Durchaus studiert, mit heißem Bemühn.

theology as "queen of the sciences" in the medieval schema. In *Urfaust*, there is yet another sequence—"I have studied and sweated my way through philosophy, medicine, and jurisprudence —and, alas, theology, too" (1–4), with the positions of law and medicine reversed at the middle of the *cursus studiorum*, but with philosophy still first and theology still last. And in the *Faustbuch* of 1587 and other early versions of the Faust legend it is explicitly stated that Faust became "a Doctor of Theology" but that then he "did not want to call himself a theologian any more, became a secular man, and called himself Doctor of Medicine."[28]

It is, however, certainly amusing, and perhaps important as well for the irony of what has with condign irony been labeled this "subversive classic,"[29] to note that by far the most comprehensive and systematic review of these four faculties does not come from Doctor Faust at all, whichever may be his own academic home base, but from his surrogate, Mephistopheles, dressed, as the stage directions specify, "in Faust's academic garb" (at 1851) and affecting a properly professorial "dry tone" (2009). After intoning the ominous theme, "If you will only despise reason and science" (1851– 67)—which will be analyzed in chapter 3—Mephistopheles-as-Faust proceeds, in response to the questions of a prospective student, to review the faculties of the university, though in a somewhat different sequence from the one in the opening words either here in *Faust* or in *Urfaust*: the first two are, as in *Faust*, philosophy and law, but the second pair are reversed, theology and then medicine. (Thus the only constant element in all three catalogs is that philosophy always comes first.)

Each of the four faculties receives the benefit of a sarcastic analysis by Mephistopheles, with at least the suggestion that the order, or at any rate the assignment of first position to philosophy, may be significant: "Make good use of time, which flies by so quickly. But a sense of proper order will teach you to save time. Therefore, my dear friend, I advise you to begin with the course in

28. Wiemken 1961, 14–15.
29. Ziolkowski 1989b, 65–79.

logic" (1908−11),[30] as the proper foundation for any of the others. This advice is followed by a hilarious review of the various Classical syllogisms and fallacies from Aristotle's *Organon*, until the student exclaims, "I do not completely understand you" (1942), and, more desperately, "It all makes me feel so stupid, as if I had a mill-wheel going around in my head" (1946−47). After logic, Mephistopheles recommends, "above everything else," the study of metaphysics, and at the crushing rate of five hours of lectures per day. For those five hours a day, the student should be prepared to listen to the professor, in accordance with the pedagogical method of the universities, "in such a way that afterwards you will be able to recognize better that he is not saying anything except what is already in the book. But you must be busy with writing it down, as though the Holy Spirit himself were dictating it to you!" (1948−63).[31]

Turning now to the second faculty, the student admits an aversion to the study of law: "I cannot bring myself to study jurisprudence." The mentor agrees, concluding that in the curriculum of the law faculties "there is never any reference to the law that is inborn within us" (1969−79), because they concentrate on positive, written law rather than on natural law.[32] In spite of his own aversion to jurisprudence, however, Faust does find it possible, from time to time in the course of the drama, to put his study of the law to good advantage. Thus when Mephistopheles explains to him at their first meeting that, as the devil, he is obliged to leave a room by the same door through which he has entered it as a poodle, Faust can ask him mockingly, "So even hell has its laws?" (1413). The third faculty is theology (of which more in a moment), while the fourth and last is medicine, which, in *Urfaust* (335) but not in *Faust*, the student declares as his (or perhaps his family's) choice of major

30. Gebraucht der Zeit, sie geht so schnell von hinnen, / Doch Ordnung lehrt Euch Zeit gewinnen. / Mein teurer Freund, ich rat' Euch drum / Zuerst Collegium Logicum.

31. Damit Ihr nachher besser seht, / Daß er nichts sagt, als was im Buche steht; / Doch Euch des Schreibens ja befleißt, / Als diktiert' Euch der Heilig' Geist!

32. Witte 1959, 81−94, and Ziolkowski 1989a, 77−78, discuss the debates over this issue at the universities of Goethe's time.

9

field: "I am to study medicine." Here in *Faust* the student asks, "Would you please say a relevant word or two also about medicine?" (2003–4). Mephistopheles obliges with a "relevant word" all right, and with a counsel of despair also about the preparation of the physician, who at best can do the patients no good and at worst can do them much harm (2011–36).

After the devil's brief parody of the study of law, the student sighs (though without an "alas"): "By now I would almost be ready to study theology!" Mephistopheles prefaces his response with a disclaimer, which is couched in typically devilish double entendre and which conflates Faust's bitter words about his father the physician, "This was the remedy, the patients died" (1048),[33] with his immediately following words about about himself the accomplice, "I myself administered the poison to thousands" (1053).[34] "I would not want to lead you astray about this science," the guidance counselor says to the neophyte. "It is so difficult here to avoid going the wrong way. There is so much poison hidden in it that it is hard to tell the poison from the cure" (1982–87).[35] Then follows a description of the two principal skills of the theologian, as the devil in his cynicism sees them. The first is what Horace called "swearing by the master's words [iurare in verba magistri],"[36] a phrase that Mephistopheles, possessing a good Classical education, quotes verbatim in German translation: "Here again the best way is to listen to only one [lecturer] and to swear by the master's words." The other indispensable skill for the theologian to cultivate is logomachy, the high art of quarreling about mere words. After the student has the temerity to express an interest in theological "concepts," he is told that these are not necessary; "for even when concepts are lacking, a word can come in at just the right time. You can battle mightily with words, construct a system out of words, believe strongly in words—and you must not diminish a single

33. Hier war die Arzenei, die Patienten starben.

34. Ich habe selbst den Gift an Tausende gegeben.

35. Ich wünschte nicht, Euch irre zu führen, / Was diese Wissenschaft betrifft, / Es ist so schwer, den falschen Weg zu meiden, / Es liegt in ihr so viel verborgnes Gift, / Und von der Arzenei ist's kaum zu unterscheiden.

36. Horace *Epistles* I.i.14.

word by a single iota" (1982–2000).[37] Faust's own lack of respect for "the word"—as he says of himself, "It is impossible for me to put such a high valuation on the word" (1226)—suggests that Mephistopheles is speaking here for Faust, or at any rate for one of the "two souls dwelling, alas, within [his] breast" (1112).

In spite of some indications that "Doctor" Faust is Doctor of Medicine,[38] therefore, it does appear plausible that he may be Doctor of Theology, too, not only in earlier versions but in Goethe's. In favor of this hypothesis there are several hints, which singly may be of varying importance but which taken together carry considerable force: the share of attention given to theology here in the Baccalaureus scene; Faust's lumping together of "doctors and masters and scribblers and clerics" (367);[39] the conjunction of the Doctor title with the subject matter of theology in the devil's sneer, "The Doctor was being catechized" (3523), which appears already in *Urfaust* (1215); the singling out of theology, among the four faculties enumerated in Faust's opening soliloquy, as the only one to receive from him the additional editorial comment of an "alas" (356); and the continuing "critique of theology" throughout.[40] Although it has been suggested that Faust's scholarly past, including therefore the academic study of theology, is forgotten after the opening scene,[41] Doctor Faust does in fact remain well informed about theological and ecclesiastical matters and takes a considerable interest in them, which suggests to one scholar that "Goethe's Faust has studied 'alas, theology, too'; and if he has also turned away from it, he has not allowed it to drop completely from his memory."[42] Or, as that same scholar has said elsewhere, commenting on Faust's credo (3432–58), "Faust's own mind is far from being untutored in the hidden subtleties of such apparently simple

37. Denn eben wo Begriffe fehlen, / Da stellt ein Wort zur rechten Zeit sich ein. / Mit Worten läßt sich trefflich streiten, / Mit Worten ein System bereiten, / An Worte läßt sich trefflich glauben, / Von einem Wort läßt sich kein Jota rauben.

38. Nager 1990, 102.

39. Doktoren, Magister, Schreiber und Pfaffen.

40. Eppelsheimer 1982, 88–92.

41. Arens 1982, 76.

42. Elizabeth M. Wilkinson in Reiss 1972, 256 n. 51.

questions. He is versed to the point of satiety in the centuries-old debates about their logical and theological status, and indicates as much when he again seems to evade the answer by putting a counter-question."[43]

Throughout the drama, moreover, Faust attracts the attention of various theological types. Several in fact put in an appearance, rather incongruously, even in the Walpurgis Night's Dream. The first is the Orthodox Theologian, with his typically orthodox (but well-grounded) suspicions regarding the identity of Mephistopheles: "There are no claws, no tail, but it is indubitable that he is a devil, as are the gods of Greece" (4271–74). Then there are the Pietists,[44] who provoke the following comment from the Crane: "I enjoy fishing in clear water or in muddy water: that is why you see a pious gentleman keeping company with devils."[45] To this the Child of the World (presumably Goethe) replies: "Yes, believe me, for such pious folk anything can become a vehicle. Even here on the Blocksberg they hold their conventicles" (4323–30),[46] suggesting that Pietists seem to be everywhere. Following immediately thereafter is the Dogmatician, whose argument is a textbook case of the logical fallacy of reasoning in a circle, also with regard to the identity of Mephistopheles: "I will not allow myself to be diverted by either criticism or doubt. The devil must be something real, for otherwise how could there be a devil?" (4343–46). A little later, there is the Chancellor, who belongs to the same camp, reacting to unconventional theological formulas with the warning: "That is no way to speak to Christians. Atheists are burned at the stake for that, because such talk is extremely dangerous. . . . The heretics and the

43. Wilkinson 1972, 131.
44. Meinhold 1958, 229–31, and Richard Brinkmann in Dürr and Molnár 1976, 167–89, discuss Goethe's relation to Pietism.
45. In dem Klaren mag ich gern / Und auch im Trüben fischen; / Darum seht ihr den frommen Herrn / Sich auch mit Teufeln mischen.
According to Goethe's comment to Eckermann, *Gespräche mit Goethe*, Part Two, 17 February 1829 (Bergemann 1987, 296), the name "Crane" is a reference to Johann Kaspar Lavater (1741–1801).
46. Ja für die Frommen, glaubet mir, / Ist alles ein Vehikel; / Sie bilden auf dem Blocksberg hier / Gar manches Konventikel.
Chiarloni 1989, 133–59, is a good general introduction.

witchmasters—they bring ruin on both the city and the country!" (4897–99, 4911–12).[47] Each is a tellingly accurate caricature of the *odium theologicum* with which Faust, if he is a Doctor of Theology, is only too well acquainted on the basis of his theological studies and from which he takes refuge in his own unconventional theologies.

In the light of Goethe's belief that "Christ has been de-mythified and secularized into a very human Jesus while institutional Christianity is regarded with a suspicious hostility,"[48] it cannot be a coincidence that so many of the references to theology and religion, here and throughout *Faust*, are spoken in such tones of caricature, satire, irony, and ridicule. Nor is this true only of the remarks that are put into the mouth of Mephistopheles. One exchange at the beginning of the drama seems to anticipate such a tone. Wagner observes, "I have often heard it said that a comedian could have something to teach a parson," to which Faust replies, "Yes, if the parson is a comedian, which might be the case from time to time" (526–29).[49] Even though Mephistopheles suggests sardonically that God himself seems to have lost his sense of humor—"The pathos of my lot ought to make you laugh," he declares, "if, that is, you had not forgotten how to" (277–78)[50]— comedy and humor are a medium for theology.[51] In a letter written five days before his death to Wilhelm von Humboldt, founder of the University of Berlin, Goethe said of *Faust*: "There is no question that it would give me infinite joy if even during my lifetime I could send *these very serious jests* [diese sehr ernsten Scherze] to my worthy, gratefully acknowledged, and widely scattered friends with my compliments, share them with them, and get their re-

47. So spricht man nicht zu Christen. / Deshalb verbrennt man Atheisten, / Weil solche Reden höchst gefährlich sind. . . . / Die Ketzer sind's! die Hexenmeister! / Und sie verderben Stadt und Land.

48. Ziolkowski 1972, 46.

49. Ich hab' es öfters rühmen hören, / Ein Komödiant könnt' einen Pfarrer lehren. / Ja, wenn der Pfarrer ein Komödiant ist; / Wie das denn wohl zu Zeiten kommen mag.

50. Mein Pathos brächte dich gewiß zum Lachen, / Hättst du dir nicht das Lachen abgewöhnt.

51. Guthke 1960, 104–9.

sponse."[52] Four months earlier he had said the same thing in greater detail, writing to Sulpiz Boisserée: "When I had placed the seal on my completed *Faust*, I still did not feel good about it. For I could not avoid the feeling that my worthiest friends, who are in general agreement with me, would not soon have the pleasure of enjoying *these seriously intended jests* [diese ernst gemeinten Scherze] for a few hours, and thus of becoming aware of what had been running around in my head and mind before it finally took on this form."[53] In this sense it is certainly accurate when Martin Greenberg, whose English translation of *Faust*, Part One, appeared in 1992, asserts: "The theology in *Faust* is one of Goethe's serious jokes."[54]

But this valid point should not be used, as it sometimes is, to trivialize these "jokes" by failing to note that they are "very serious" and that they were "seriously intended."[55] This applies in special measure to the theology: it is Mephistopheles, not God, who has the last word in the Prologue in Heaven (350–53), but it is God's own Chorus Mysticus who have the last word in the drama (12104–11). And He who laughs last does laugh best[56]— regardless of what Mephistopheles may think of the Lord's sense of humor (277–78). The treatment in the drama of what has been called "the devouring materialism of the Church"[57] aptly illustrates the special quality of the theological irony. Mephistopheles quotes the words of Margarete's parish priest upon being shown the jewel box: "That was the right thing to do, for there is great gain in overcoming [temptation]. The church has a strong stomach, and it has swallowed entire countries without ever overeating. Only the

52. Goethe to Wilhelm von Humboldt, 17 March 1832 (Trunz 1968, 460); italics added.

53. Goethe to Sulpiz Boisserée, 24 November 1831 (Trunz 1968, 458); italics added.

54. Greenberg 1992, xiv.

55. Meyer 1970 is a brief but bold and provocative effort to read Part Two of *Faust* in the light of Goethe's phrase and of his use of "jest [Scherz]" elsewhere in his writings.

56. Guthke 1960, 104–11, has compared Goethe and Milton in this respect.

57. Atkins 1958, 73.

church, my dear ladies, can digest ill-gotten gains" (2834–40).[58] The motif resurfaces in the confrontation of the Archbishop and the Emperor at the end of Part Two, Act IV, over the dangers of being in league with the devil, a scene that is filled with ironic references to the penance by which the Emperor is to pay up "by giving back to the sanctuary a pittance from [his] tainted fortune" (10991–92), thereby making everything right with the church and with God. Nevertheless the irony makes a serious and valid point. For all his greed and hypocrisy, the Archbishop has identified the precise evil that Faust must shake off if he is ever to recover his freedom and humanity, as Faust himself acknowledges at the beginning of the next act: "If I could only put magic far out of my path, utterly unlearn the formulas of sorcery, and stand in thy presence, O Nature, just as a man, that would make it worthwhile to be a human being" (11404–7).[59] Similarly, an earlier confrontation over theology, the pious but naive "catechizing" (3523) of Faust by Margarete, is at one level certainly "a jest." That is, moreover, how Faust treats it, with his cavalier declaration of tolerance, "I have no intention of robbing people of their feelings and their church" (3420), and his no less cavalier declaration of anticlerical intolerance, "If you ask such questions of the priests or sages, their answer seems to make fun of the questioner" (3428–30). But at another level it is, in Margarete's eyes, "seriously intended," as she sighs, "One has to believe in this," and "Oh, if I only could make an impression on you!" (3421–22). And once again it is, in the event, her seriousness that prevails over the cynicism of both Faust and Mephistopheles, in the eschatological denouement of the drama. Therefore, even with due attention to all of the ironies that have so preoccupied recent readers, it would

58. So ist man recht gesinnt! / Wer überwindet, der gewinnt. / Die Kirche hat einen guten Magen, / Hat ganze Länder aufgefressen, / Und doch noch nie sich übergessen; / Die Kirch' allein, meine lieben Frauen, / Kann ungerechtes Gut verdauen.

59. Könnt' ich Magie von meinem Pfad entfernen, / Die Zaubersprüche ganz und gar verlernen, / Stünd' ich, Natur, vor dir ein Mann allein, / Da wär's der Mühe wert, ein Mensch zu sein.

appear to be, at the very least, one legitimate reading of that denouement to ask what it was that the genius of Gustav Mahler found so exalted in it and that he celebrated so sublimely by juxtaposing it with the medieval hymn *Veni Creator Spiritus* in his Eighth Symphony.[60] Of this "full-scale musical context [of] the *Veni Creator Spiritus* and [of] the belief in immortality voiced by Goethe in the final scene of *Faust,*" Bruno Walter declared, on the basis of a profound knowledge of Mahler both personal and musical coupled with a profound knowledge of Goethe's works, "No other work [by Mahler] expresses so fully the impassioned 'Yes' to life."[61]

In the theodicy that pervades Goethe's *Faust* one scholar has found "in accordance with Goethe's intention, an intersection between the religious element of a predestined justification of Faust before God and the dramatic element of the alternatives of damnation or salvation, an intersection that has not yet been resolved."[62] The eschatology represented by the outcome of that tension between predestination and free will is the ultimate irony of Faust's victory over a power "that constantly intends to do evil and constantly does good" (1335–36).[63] In this respect as in many others, Goethe's *Faust* seems to resemble an earlier "seriously intended jest" in the grand style, and one that was explicitly identified as a "comedy," Dante's *Divine Comedy*.[64] There is, however, at least one significant difference, pointed out long ago by one of the earliest and most discerning readers of *Faust,* Carl Gustav Carus, in a letter dated 26 December 1834: "And have you not often in spirit drawn the parallels between the great work of Dante and this work of Goethe? Except that in the former the most painful and the most blessed conditions of the soul pass by the viewer (which is why it is called a 'spectacle,' *Divine Comedy*), whereas in the latter the

60. Floros 1977, 46–53, 129–32; also the discussion "Monotheismus oder Pantheismus," 118–22, and "Christliche Dogmatik und Glaubenslehre," 122–25.
61. Walter 1958, 107–8.
62. J. Müller 1969, 155.
63. . . . die stets das Böse will und stets das Gute schafft.
64. The parallel is drawn by Friedrich Schelling, in Hamlin 1976, 438, and examined by Wordsworth 1919, 1–27.

protagonist is constantly being moved and must restlessly pass through all the anguish and joy of life."[65]

A Dantean story line is adumbrated more than once in the two prologues to the drama. At the conclusion of the Prelude on the Stage, the Director, authorizing the use of elaborate stage props and machines, prescribes the following for the drama: "So within the confines of this house of boards you can stride through the whole circle of creation, and with deliberate speed you can wander from heaven through the world to hell" (239–42).[66] It seems unlikely that, as some interpreters maintain, the sequence in this final line, "from heaven through the world to hell," represents Goethe's original intention about Faust's eternal destiny; it has even been suggested that it belongs not here at all but actually to Goethe's version of *The Magic Flute*.[67] Yet this line does suggest "an illuminating relationship with the end of Part Two."[68] For in fact, of course, Faust does "stride" (albeit with something less than "deliberate speed") not, as the Director imagines, "from heaven through the world to hell," but "from the world through hell to heaven"— the very path traversed by Dante the pilgrim.[69] The course of that "wandering" constitutes the plot of *Faust*, which is therefore a narrative of development and growth, a theme that is important for Goethe's understanding both of the individual and of history.[70] Thus *Faust* is, to allude yet again to Dante, a narrative of pilgrimage. The leitmotif of pilgrimage, development, and growth reappears in the Prologue in Heaven, where the verbs employed are not "wandering [wandeln]" but "straying [irren]" and "striving [streben]." "Man will stray, as long as he goes on striving" is the Lord's own formulation of the leitmotif (317).[71] Already in this

65. Carus 1937, 26.

66. So schreitet in dem engen Bretterhaus / Den ganzen Kreis der Schöpfung aus / Und wandelt mit bedächt'ger Schnelle / Vom Himmel durch die Welt zur Hölle.

67. Seidlin 1949, 468n.

68. Bennett 1986, 58.

69. The parallels between the closing scenes of *Faust* and of the *Divine Comedy* are the subject of brief but telling comments by Hamlin 1976, 307 n. 6.

70. Heise 1976, 116–38.

71. Es irrt der Mensch, solang' er strebt.

passage, Mephistopheles, as becomes his wont throughout Part One, calls Faust "Doctor." But the Lord God identifies Faust instead as his "servant [Knecht]" (299), which is what Faust remains through all the changes and chances of his "straying" and "striving." As the Lord God says of him, in anticipation of the teleology many thousands of lines later, "Even though he serves me now in a confused manner, I shall soon lead him into the light. When the tree is in leaf, the gardener knows that there will be flower and fruit to adorn the years to come" (308–11)—the "soon" in those words being meant no more literally than the "with deliberate speed" in the Director's.[72]

Therefore, despite all the "confusion," the sorcery and witchcraft and downright blasphemy (1583–1606) into which he "strays" in the course of his "wandering" and "striving," Faust is being led "into the light" and retains at his core a deep sense of reverence, a sense that Mephistopheles finds incomprehensible but that Faust continues to affirm: "The capacity for awe is the best feature of humanity. The world may extract a heavy payment for such feelings, but someone who has been stirred feels the Numinous profoundly" (6272–74).[73] It is a capacity for awe in the presence of the Numinous from which, "when he is most powerfully touched at the very depths of his existence,"[74] Faust is never altogether alienated. The numinous objects of Faust's sense of awe and reverence, however, do not remain the same. One permissible way to read the drama, therefore, would seem to be to watch the development, the "wandering," the "straying," and the "striving," in relation to these objects of reverence, and thus to see *Faust* as a kind of bildungsroman (for which the definition "apprenticeship novel" has been proposed).[75] What has been observed about the differ-

72. Wenn er mir jetzt auch nur verworren dient, / So werd' ich ihn bald in die Klarheit führen. / Weiß doch der Gärtner, wenn das Bäumchen grünt, / Daß Blüt' und Frucht die künft'gen Jahre zieren. Zezschwitz 1985, 206–9, comments on these lines.

73. Das Schaudern ist der Menschheit bestes Teil; / Wie auch die Welt ihm das Gefühl verteure, / Ergriffen, fühlt er tief das Ungeheure.

74. May 1962, 86.

75. Shaffner 1984, 3–5.

ences and similarities between Christoph Martin Wieland's *Agathon* and Goethe's *Wilhelm Meister's Apprenticeship* could be applied also to a comparison of *Wilhelm Meister* and *Faust*, which "looks very different indeed" from Goethe's novel; "however," as has been said, "the marked differences in type of setting, narrative manner, and understanding of human psychology between the two [works] conceal a profound affinity."[76] Thus "*Faust* and *Wilhelm Meister* are the working out of this odyssey in poetry and in prose," respectively, in which Goethe gave expression to his idea of the *Bildungstrieb*, the impulse and instinct for creative development.[77]

Goethe himself provided a typological framework within which to chart Faust's theological Bildungstrieb, in an aphorism that has been my longtime favorite among the epigrams collected in the *Maxims and Reflections* compiled from various of his writings, letters, and other fragments:[78] "When we do natural science, we are pantheists; when we do poetry, we are polytheists; when we moralize, we are monotheists."[79] The epigram actually derives from a letter Goethe originally wrote to Fritz Jacobi dated 6 January 1813: "For my part, I cannot be satisfied, amid the manifold directions of my being, with only one way of thinking. As a poet and an artist, I am a polytheist; on the other hand, I am a pantheist as a natural scientist—and one of these as decisively as the other. And if I have need for one God for my personality as a moral man, that, too, is provided for."[80]

76. Beddow 1982, 63; on the role of "irony" also in Goethe's novel, the observations of Swales 1978, 70–72.

77. Spranger 1946, 32–34.

78. Hecker 1907 is still the most thorough and careful investigation of this underutilized collection.

79. *Maximen und Reflexionen,* # 807: "Wir sind naturforschend Pantheisten, dichtend Polytheisten, sittlich Monotheisten." Both the letter and the maxim are quoted in Buchwald 1964 and in Thielicke 1982, but they are not used as interpretive keys.

80. Ich für mich kann, bei den mannigfaltigen Richtungen meines Wesens, nicht an einer Denkweise genug haben; als Dichter und Künstler bin ich Polytheist, Pantheist hingegen als Naturforscher, und eins so entschieden als das andre. Bedarf ich eines [i.e., "e i n e s," not "eines"] Gottes für meine Persönlichkeit, als sittlicher Mensch, so ist dafür auch gesorgt.

Mason 1967, 362. It will be evident that I diverge from Mason's translation of "eines" as "a" rather than as "one."

It deserves to be noted that within the range of the three "ways of thinking" distinguished by Goethe there is no mention of the fourth possibility, atheism.[81] And the same appears to be true of Faust, who falls into despair and who even seems to contemplate suicide (720–36, 1579–80), but who does not appear to consider the atheist alternative. This is because "in reality, Goethe's Faust has not in any way renounced God. . . . Therefore Faust is a God-seeker, not a God-denier."[82] As Faust says to Margarete in his credo, "Who can perceive God and then presume to say: 'I do not believe in him'? The All-comprehending, the All-preserving, does he not sustain and embrace you and me and himself?" (3435–41).[83] The debate over which was preferable, atheism or superstition, had been raging up to Goethe's time.[84] Yet, in the face of all the superstition swirling around him and sometimes within him, Faust does not seem to consider atheism; when it appears at all in the text, atheism is seen as a polemical device rather than as an existential option (4898). Goethe's contemporaries and critics may have equated his "pantheism" and "Spinozism" with "atheism,"[85] but he did not. At one place in *Dichtung und Wahrheit*, reacting to the mystical theology of his Swiss contemporary, Johann Caspar Lavater, and echoing the words of a letter he had written to Lavater already in 1782, he did exclaim: "All unsuccessful attempts at conversion leave him who has been selected for a proselyte stubborn and obdurate; and this was especially the case with me when Lavater at last came out with the hard dilemma,—'Either Christian or atheist!' Upon this I declared that, if he would not leave me my own Christianity as I had hitherto cherished it, I could readily decide for Atheism, particularly as I saw that nobody knew precisely what either meant."[86]

81. The comments of Rintelen 1950, 7–19, are brief but appropriate.
82. Hering 1952, 43.
83. Wer [darf Gott] empfinden, / Und sich unterwinden / Zu sagen: ich glaub' ihn nicht? / Der Allumfasser, / Der Allerhalter, / Faßt und erhält er nicht / Dich, mich, sich selbst?
84. Pelikan 1971–89, 5:66–67, 180–81.
85. Boyle 1991, 1:282–85.
86. Goethe, *Dichtung und Wahrheit*, III, 14.

But that polemical comment is still a long way from placing atheism as an option on the same level alongside pantheism, polytheism, and monotheism, as is clear also from his comment earlier in Book Three of *Dichtung und Wahrheit* about French atheism: "How hollow and empty did we feel in this melancholy, atheistic half-night, in which Earth vanished with all its images, Heaven with all its stars."[87]

There is another, not inconsiderable reason for "privileging" (to invoke a term that, used as a verb, seems to have become almost mandatory in literary studies) this typology of pantheist, polytheist, monotheist: it comes from Goethe himself, rather than from Marx or Freud or, for that matter, the Bible or the Christian theological tradition; and there would seem to be some degree of prima facie plausibility to any schematism that is the author's own. Although he was not applying it explicitly to his treatment of the legend and character of Faust, he evidently did see in it a kind of theological taxonomy, according to which there was a correlation evident between the particular activity and task in which his own mind and spirit were engaged and the one or another particular view of the Divine to which he was just then committed. In the letter to Jacobi of 1813, Goethe invoked this taxonomy for a highly personal credo about his own view of the Divine (or, rather, views of the Divine) and about how each of the major tasks of his lifework—as poet and artist, as natural scientist, and as moral man (and in that order)— was correlated with an appropriate "Denkweise." But when the section "From the Literary Remains" was anthologized from his letters and other works for the *Maxims and Reflections*, not only was the order changed—from polytheism/pantheism/monotheism to pantheism/polytheism/monotheism—but the pronoun was also changed from the first person singular to the first person plural, thus raising it from the status of a personal confession (which it obviously is, and remains) to that of a philosophical and theological generalization; as their editor says of the sayings collected in the *Maxims and Reflections*, "the sense is generalized, refined, deepened."[88] And if this maxim is a valid generalization for Goethe and not a casual or purely idiosyncratic notion, to whom should it apply more fittingly than the character of Faust? There is, moreover, a genetic case to be made for its application to Faust. For the three periods of his development in the drama correspond to the sequence of Goethe's writing, beginning with the early "pantheistic" sections belonging to the author's original conception, continuing with the "polytheism" of Walpurgis Night and Classical Walpurgis Night as written in the first quarter of the 1800s, and closing with the "monotheism" of the sections written near the end of Goethe's life. Quoting the words of Goethe's letter to Jacobi, one critic has urged that "the close of *Faust* is the best evidence of how these words are meant," a judgment that the following exposition shares, despite its sharp differences from the interpretation that he has given.[89]

There is, of course, a great danger that in the application of any such typology, even one of Goethe's minting, to so multifaceted a work as Goethe's *Faust* its categories will do violence to the complexity of the drama and its characters. The director in the Prelude at the Theater speaks about the drama as "a sort of ragout" (100), and Faust uses the same word in the opening scene (539): a ragout cannot have only one ingredient. There is an even greater danger: to forget that in Goethe's formulation, both in the letter to Jacobi and in the *Maxims and Reflections*, these three categories of "ways of thinking" are not distinguished from one another chronologically, and that they are not meant to be mutually exclusive; any such schematism would do violence to what have been called "the varying modes of Goethe's thought."[90] Rather, the categories are distinguished from one another, so to speak, vocationally and psychologically. As Faust moves from one vocation to another, he seems to manifest many of the features of the way of thinking and theological worldview with which that vocation is associated in Goethe's maxim. Precisely because the distinction is not meant to

88. Hecker 1907, xxviii.
89. Möbus 1964, 309.
90. Wilkinson and Willoughby 1962, 132–52.

be chronological, some features of one of these vocations will manifest themselves also within the context of another: Faust the poetic artist retains the natural scientist's interest in Nature, in geology and optics, and especially in applied physics and marine engineering, until just before the end of the drama,[91] and Faust the moral philosopher has at least somewhat intimated this concern from the beginning of the drama. As this is true of these three vocations of natural scientist, poetic artist, and moral philosopher, so it also applies to the theological worldviews of "natural scientist as pantheist" and of "poetic artist as polytheist," together with that of "moral philosopher as monotheist."

Nor is this merely because Faust, like Goethe, cannot be content with one way but must come to terms with "the manifold directions of [his] being." Rather, the species of morality, and thus the definition of monotheism, through which Faust finds salvation, though it transcends both his scientific pantheism and his poetic polytheism, does so not by negating either of them but by fulfilling both of them and making them sublime. What Goethe said in his diary on 30 June 1830, while studying the literary fragments of his youth, would also apply to the person of Faust: "The truth, but undeveloped, so that it can be regarded as error." Every effort to make Goethe's *Faust* into a "Christian" drama in any orthodox or traditional sense has found itself blocked by that conjunction. As two of the prayers in the closing scene put it, both of them addressed by the Doctor Marianus to the Virgin Mary: "Let every nobler intent be placed at thy service!" (12100–12101);[92] and "Grant approval to that which moves this man's breast, so earnestly and tenderly, and which it now bears before thy presence with the holy desire of love" (12001–4).[93] These nobler intents, higher aspirations, and earnest yearnings are the expressions of an intellectual and spiritual "Eros, which started everything" (8479) and which finds fulfillment in God. Goethe's younger contemporary,

91. Jockers 1957, 106–18: "Die ästhetische Stufe."

92. Werde jeder beßre Sinn / Dir zum Dienst erbötig!

93. Billige, was des Mannes Brust / Ernst und zart beweget / Und mit heiliger Liebeslust / Dir entgegenträget.

the Danish philosopher Søren Kierkegaard, likewise distinguished three categories or, as they are sometimes translated into English, "existence-spheres": the aesthetic, the ethical, and the religious. Because the title of the work in which Kierkegaard most fully developed that distinction is translated into English as *Stages on Life's Way*, these three are usually called "stages."[94] Kierkegaard's stages are not strictly chronological either, but in his philosophy of religion and his theology they are, ultimately, mutually opposed. If Goethe's "ways of thinking" are to be employed in any analogous way as "stages [Stufen]" or, in a term he sometimes used, as "stages of development [Bildungstufen],"[95] on the contrary, they must be seen as developmental but dialectical, and therefore as inter-penetrating one another; and that is how they are being employed here to interpret Goethe's *Faust.*

94. Thomte 1948, especially 16–109, is a careful analysis of the distinctions and of the interrelations between the three "stages."
95. Rowley 1983, 44–66.

CHAPTER TWO

The Natural Scientist as Pantheist

WHETHER HE is a Doctor of Theology or not, Doctor Faust definitely is a scientist, both in the general sense of "science" as it is being used here to render "Wissenschaft" as a comprehensive term for learning and scholarship also in the humanities and social sciences (1851) and in the more usual present-day sense of "science" to refer specifically to "Naturwissenschaft."[1] And therefore, in keeping with the epigram of Goethe that forms the organizing principle of this book, "When we do natural science, we are pantheists," Doctor Faust the natural scientist is also Doctor Faust the pantheistic theologian.[2]

Faust's scientific vocation makes itself evident in his opening scene, which takes place, according to the stage directions, "in a high-vaulted, narrow Gothic chamber" (at 354). The action returns to that setting in Part Two, Act I: "high-vaulted, narrow Gothic room, which was formerly Faust's and is unchanged" (at 6566). Apparently adjoining this room—since Mephistopheles is described as "entering" (at 6831)—there is, however, a "medieval-style laboratory," which has "pieces of extensive but not very

---

1. The titles in Schmid 1940 and the essays in Amrine, Zucker, and Wheeler 1987 examine the several sciences individually.

2. Michael Böhler in Wittkowski 1984, 313–35, is a provocative discussion.

helpful apparatus intended for fantastic purposes" (6819). The text does not specify this in so many words, but it does seem plausible, in the light of the stage direction that the room is "unchanged" (at 6566), that the "medieval-style laboratory," as well as at least some "pieces of extensive but not very helpful apparatus intended for fantastic purposes," must be there already when Faust occupies the suite, or perhaps even when his father and his forebears before him occupied it. As Faust sighs, "Surrounded on all sides by glasses and beakers, jammed with instruments, and crowded with my ancestors' furniture—that is your world! What a world!" (406–9).[3] For in Faust's Gothic study there are various pieces of scientific apparatus and various scientific supplies, including a vial of poison (690–701). He does have some leftover apparatus from his father in his study (676–77), presumably as part of the experiments with medical alchemy in which the father had been engaged (1034–45). These experiments were, like some of the equipment in the laboratory, "extensive" enough, but were ultimately (using the euphemistic litotes) "not very helpful," because, as Faust says, "This was the remedy, the patients died" (1048). As "a disillusioned physicist," to invoke the striking phrase of the physicist Werner Heisenberg in commenting on this passage,[4] Faust also speaks of some of his own scientific "instruments," which were intended to be keys to truth but which now mock him (668–71). Close by are skeletons, both animal and human (416–17). A little later, when Faust is alone, he addresses a human skull: "Why are you sneering at me, you hollow skull, except to tell me that your brain, like mine, was once bewildered in search of the light of day?" (664–66).[5] When Mephistopheles returns to Faust's study in Part Two, the skulls are still there (6613).

All these skulls, skeletons, and other scientific apparatus and supplies are props in support of Faust's "scientific patterns of

3. Mit Gläsern, Büchsen rings umstellt, / Mit Instrumenten vollgepfropft, / Urväter-Hausrat drein gestopft— / Das ist deine Welt! das heißt eine Welt!

4. Heisenberg 1967, 31.

5. Was grinsest du mir, hohler Schädel, her, / Als daß dein Hirn wie meines einst verwirret / Den leichten Tag gesucht . . . ?

thought," his scientific vocation and mind-set.[6] It is a mind-set born of the dialogue with the scientific tradition; Goethe's *Theory of Colors* has been called "the first history of scientific method."[7] But Faust's natural science has been made possible by an intellectual maturity that has gone beyond the authority of that tradition. Thus when, early in Part Two, in the Great Hall, the order is issued, "Let there be multi-colored fantasies blooming to match the fashion of the day, let their form be wondrous and strange, unlike anything that Nature has ever evolved" (5144–47), or when in that context the Nosegay of Phantasy declares of itself, "Theophrastus would not dare to tell you my name" (5136–37), referring to Theophrastus, the pupil of Aristotle and author of two major works of botanical taxonomy[8]—these are the celebration of a scientific evolution, first in Nature herself but then in the knowledge of Nature as well, that has transcended the conventional boundaries of the past, as it has in Faust's own thought and work. This attitude makes its presence felt, for example, in the controversy over the origin of all things between Thales and Anaxagoras, the pre-Socratic natural scientists and philosophers, which is summarized with considerable scientific detail in a scholarly "agon or debate" that takes up precisely a hundred lines of the Classical Walpurgis Night (7851–7950).[9] The controversy is then echoed near the end of that scene when Thales exclaims: "Hail! Hail! Once again! How happy I am in full bloom, saturated with the Beautiful and the True. . . . Everything emerged from the water!!" (8432–35).[10] Goethe the natural scientist regarded this controversy between the Vulcanist, who looked upon fire as the primal element, and the Neptunist, who taught that everything came from water—as that controversy is represented here by Anaxagoras and Thales,

6. D. Lohmeyer 1975, 15–20.

7. E. Heller 1952, 10.

8. On his relation to Aristotle, see the extensive footnote in W. Jaeger 1948, 115–16.

9. Commentary by D. Lohmeyer 1975, 253–59, and a brief note by Atkins 1954, 76.

10. Heil! Heil! aufs neue! / Wie ich mich blühend freue, / Vom Schönen, Wahren durchdrungen . . . / Alles ist aus dem Wasser entsprungen!!

respectively—as a scientific equivalent of the doctrinal controversies between religious denominations.[11] The treatment of the scientific heritage of Classical antiquity here suggests, therefore, that Faust's view of scientific research in relation to the history of the natural sciences is an especially powerful instance of the attitude toward tradition he has voiced early on: "What you have as heritage, now take as task, for thus you will make it your own" (682–83).[12] These words seem to be directed to all tradition, because none of it truly is one's own until and unless it has been gained anew instead of being merely inherited; but in the context they do have special relevance to the history of the natural sciences.

Although the emphasis of the opening monologues lies on Faust's profound disappointment and frustration with scientific pursuit and on his eagerness to try something new—of which more in chapter 3—that presupposes that he has been engaged in the pursuit over a period of years (360–63). The ideal of that pursuit, at any rate before the impasse into which Faust has come, is glowingly described in Goethe's autobiographical words, quoted by Johann Peter Eckermann as having been spoken just at the time when *Faust* was being completed: "There is nothing to surpass the joy that the study of Nature provides for us. Her secrets have an unfathomable depth, but we human beings have the permission and the opportunity to look at them ever increasingly. And precisely because she remains unfathomable to the end, she has for us the eternal charm that we can go to her over and over and try out new insights and new discoveries over and over."[13]

As for Goethe himself, therefore, as Eckermann put it six years earlier, when Goethe was seventy-five years old: "He can never get his fill of investigating and experiencing. In none of his directions is he finished and done. He always wants to go further, ever further! always learning, always learning! And thereby he shows

11. Eckermann, *Gespräche mit Goethe*, Part Three, 18 May 1824 (Bergemann 1987, 516).

12. Was du ererbt von deinen Vätern hast, / Erwirb es, um es zu besitzen.

13. Eckermann, *Gespräche mit Goethe*, Part Three, 15 July 1831 (Bergemann 1987, 708).

himself to be a man of eternal and totally inexhaustible youth."[14] Eckermann likewise supplies something of an explanation for the advice that Mephistopheles, disguised as Faust, gives to an eager but callow youth who expresses boundless ambition and intellectual hubris, which is an ironic though telling caricature of Faust's (and Goethe's) scholarly career: "I would like to become really learned and to comprehend everything in Earth and Heaven, all of science and all of Nature" (1898–1901). To which the diabolical admissions adviser replies that if he truly is intent on becoming "really learned," he is "on the right track," but be must be careful not "to let himself be scattered" (1902–3). For, according to Eckermann, Goethe concluded on the basis of his own experience that it was—or, by hindsight, would have been in his case—"finally the highest art, to learn to limit and isolate yourself";[15] and a few months earlier he had warned, also on the basis of his experience: "Above all, protect yourself against fragmentation, and hold your powers together."[16] Goethe was applying this combination of regret and advice not only to his work as a writer but to his scientific research, as well as to the ambiguities of his experience as an impresario and public figure.

Faust's bitter disillusionment with this attitude toward research in the natural sciences helps to set up the plot of the tragedy; but before we consider that, there are at least three basic components of his scientific mind-set that do merit closer examination here, also because of their implications for the eventual resolution of the tragedy. One of these is mockingly described by Mephistopheles, when he calls Doctor Faust a man "who has utter contempt for the word, and who spurns outward appearances to pay attention only to the profundity of beings" (1328–30). Words are not enough for Faust either as natural scientist or as philosopher (or as theologian)—as he says already in *Urfaust*, he wants "not to be

14. Eckermann, *Gespräche mit Goethe*, Part Three, 16 April 1825 (Bergemann 1987, 534).

15. Eckermann, *Gespräche mit Goethe*, Part One, 20 April 1825 (Bergemann 1987, 143).

16. Eckermann, *Gespräche mit Goethe*, Part One, 3 December 1824 (Bergemann 1987, 118).

confined to words any longer" (32)—because "now it is time to demonstrate by deeds that the dignity of a man need not shrink from divine heights" (712–13);[17] for the divine aspirations of the human spirit, actions do speak louder than words. As Goethe said in *Wilhelm Meister,* "There are only a few who have the vision and at the same time are capable of the deed. The vision is broadening, but crippling; the deed is enlivening, but limiting."[18] Spurning "the word" in favor of "the deed" not only in his natural science but even in his translation of the Greek term *logos* in the New Testament (1220–37), Faust has repeatedly shown his fascination both with "deeds" and with "the profundity of beings." He shrugs off the pedantry of those who would substitute the artificiality of the written word for the reality of the world and of Nature (1716, 1720–21). Such pedantry finds its fitting spokesman in Wagner, his academic assistant, who, in response to Faust's worship of the sun as a "goddess" at the time of the "twilight glow" (1070–99), makes it clear what interests him and what does not: "I have often had some wierd moments, but that desire is one I have never experienced. Looking at woods and fields palls very quickly. I do not envy the bird its ability to fly. How different are the pleasures of the mind, going from book to book and from page to page! Winter nights acquire a chaste beauty, and a sense of well-being warms every limb. Why, with a worthwhile parchment unrolled before you, heaven itself stoops down to be with you" (1100–1109).[19]

For Wagner, apparently, when you have seen one sunset, you have seen them all, but it is not so with books. Faust, by contrast, is surrounded by thousands of books (661), but he knows how fatuous and ultimately sterile a view of the world and of knowledge derived

17. Hier ist es Zeit, durch Taten zu beweisen, / Daß Manneswürde nicht der Götterhöhe weicht.

18. *Wilhelm Meister,* VIII, 5.

19. Ich hatte selbst oft grillenhafte Stunden, / Doch solchen Trieb hab' ich noch nie empfunden. / Man sieht sich leicht an Wald und Feldern satt; / Des Vogels Fittich werd' ich nie beneiden. / Wie anders tragen uns die Geistesfreuden / Von Buch zu Buch, von Blatt zu Blatt! / Da werden Winternächte hold und schön, / Ein selig Leben wärmet alle Glieder, / Und ach! entrollst du gar ein würdig Pergamen, / So steigt der ganze Himmel zu dir nieder.

only from book learning can be. As he asks Wagner in *Urfaust*, alluding to the promise of Christ, "Is the parchment the holy well from which one drink will quench the thirst forever? You have not found true refreshment unless it flows to you from out of your own soul" (213–16).[20] In the final version he seems to acknowledge to Wagner, whether seriously or ironically, that he is caught between the two, and that at least on one level he almost envies Wagner his simpleminded bookishness: "You are conscious of only one drive. Oh, may you never come to know the other one! In my own breast, alas, there are two souls dwelling that do not want to stay together. One of them holds on with life and limb to this world, in coarse sensuality, while the other is straining to break free from the dust and to rise to the abodes of the blest" (1110–17).[21] But when he goes on to speak to Mephistopheles about "my breast, which has been healed of the drive for knowledge" (1768), he would seem to be referring specifically to the narrow "drive for knowledge" of the detached natural scientist who is imprisoned in his laboratory and of the dry-as-dust scholar who cannot escape from his library.

For as a student of Nature, Faust has been engaged all along in quite another kind of "drive for knowledge," the scientific quest for the underlying elements of cosmological reality, beyond the empirical data of observation and experimentation; and from that he has not been "healed" and never will be.[22] Near the beginning of the drama, Faust's "invocation of the four" leads to an explanation of what "the four" are—namely, the "elements" of fire, water, air, and earth—adding: "Anyone who would not be acquainted with the elements, their powers and their properties, could not be master of the spirits" (1272–82). Not only "stuff" as material reality, but even "the spirits" as spiritual reality, are unintelligible apart from

20. Das Pergament, ist das der heilge Bronnen, / Woraus ein Trunk den Durst auf ewig stillt [John 4:14]? / Erquickung hast du nicht gewonnen, / Wenn sie dir nicht aus eigner Seele quillt.

21. Du bist dir nur des einen Triebs bewußt; / O lerne nie den andern kennen! / Zwei Seelen wohnen, ach! in meiner Brust, / Die eine will sich von der andern trennen; / Die eine hält, in derber Liebeslust, / Sich an die Welt mit klammernden Organen; / Die andre hebt gewaltsam sich vom Dust / Zu den Gefilden hoher Ahnen.

22. Dzialas 1939, 141–63.

these "elements." In fact, three of the four (fire as present in the sun, earth, and air) are, in that order, the topics of the hymns of the three archangels, Raphael, Gabriel, and Michael, respectively, at the opening of the Prologue in Heaven, with water also putting in an appearance through a reference to the sea (243–66). Thus Faust is engaged in continuing the scientific-philosophical investigations of the Greeks into the *stoicheia,* documented in the *Theaetetus* and the *Timaeus* of Plato but going back in its roots to the pre-Socratics.[23] His first attempt to apply the concept, in his seriocomical encounter with the poodle, ends in failure, because "None of the four is in the beast," necessitating a formula of imprecation appropriate to a demonic being, a "fugitive from hell" that does not belong to this universe of the four elements (1292–99). The preoccupation with the stoicheia, moreover, continues in later parts of the drama. The Classical Walpurgis Night closes—appropriately enough, considering the Classical origins of the four—with an apostrophe to all of them, individually and collectively: "Hail to the sea! Hail to the waves, glowing with the sacred fire! Hail to the water! Hail to the fire! Hail to this rare adventure! Hail to the gentle breezes! Hail to the mysterious caves! Let all four elements be celebrated in this place!" (8480–87).[24] There is another apostrophe to them after the death of Euphorion and Helen (9981–82, 9992–10016). But for now, that quest for the stocheia, too, has issued in total frustration for Faust as pantheist and natural scientist: "I can feel it now: it was in vain that I assembled for myself all the treasures of the human spirit. For now when I finally set myself down, there is no new power welling up within me. I am not even a hair's breadth taller than I was, and no nearer to the Infinite" (1810–15),[25] even though "the Infinite" has been, at the cost of

23. Plato *Theaetetus* 201e; *Timaeus* 48b.

24. Heil dem Meere! Heil den Wogen, / Von dem heiligen Feuer umzogen! / Heil dem Wasser! Heil dem Feuer! / Heil dem seltnen Abenteuer! / Heil den mildgewogenen Lüften! / Heil geheimnisreichen Grüften! / Hochgefeiert seid allhier, / Element' ihr alle vier!

25. Ich fühl's, vergebens hab' ich alle Schätze / Des Menschengeists auf mich herbeigerafft, / Und wenn ich mich am Ende niedersetze, / Quillt innerlich doch keine neue Kraft; / Ich bin nicht um ein Haar breit höher, / Bin dem Unendlichen nicht näher.

"all the treasures of the human spirit," the ultimate object of both his scientific research and his pantheistic devotion.

A second characteristic of Faust's scientific outlook is an explicitly practical interest, which carries over even into his philological science as a New Testament scholar, in a scene in which "Faust is allowed to be preoccupied with a traditional theological problem despite his already unambiguously expressed disbelief in Christian revelation."[26] When Faust's spiritual turmoil, combined with his interest in philological science, "impels [him] to consult the fundamental text and to give an honest try to translate the sacred original into [his] beloved German," imitating the example of Martin Luther on the Wartburg in 1521, the text he chooses is the opening verse of the Gospel of John, which, during the history of the medieval theology that Faust has "studied [his] way all through" (356–57), has probably been the subject of more metaphysical speculation than any other passage in the New Testament.[27] Faust tries out three possible translations of logos before settling on the one he takes to be correct. The first one, and the most common and obvious one, is "word [das Wort]," but this he rejects summarily with the objection: "It is impossible for me to value the word that highly: I must translate it some other way"; for as he says elsewhere, "A name is only sound and smoke" (3457), and nothing more. That brings him to the translation "mind [der Sinn]," but this, too, is unacceptable, in the light of the cosmic power attributed to the person of the Logos in the text of the Gospel: "Is it the mind that accomplishes everything and creates everything?" On that score, he goes on, "power [die Kraft]" would seem to be more nearly adequate, but "something is already warning me not to stick with that." The "something" that warned him, he continues, was nothing less than "the Spirit [der Geist]." With that help, he now finds the solution: "The Spirit is assisting me! All at once I see the answer, and I write down confidently: In the beginning was the deed [die Tat]!" (1220–37).[28] That emphasis on the deed as divine

26. Atkins 1952, 370; historical comments in Boyle 1981, 196–213.
27. Rosenfeld 1962, 178–205, illumines this episode from the medieval background.
28. On Faust as translator, Görner 1989, 119–32.

is fully in keeping with his character throughout, from the declaration of his introductory monologue, "Now it is time to demonstrate by deeds that the dignity of a man need not shrink from divine heights" (712–13),[29] to his declaration near the end of the drama, that there was still room on the Earth for doing great deeds (10181–82).[30] And therefore: "In the beginning was the deed!" Thus "the translation has moved with almost systematic precision from the word *logos* to its very opposite,"[31] an indication of just how radically Faust takes the imperative of his own injunction about tradition as task (682–83).

Hence the ideal of "Knowledge Its Own End," as articulated by Cardinal Newman in Discourse V of his *Idea of a University,* seems foreign to Faust, whose pathetically voiced "melancholia" and self-criticism, "What one does not know is what one could use, and what one does know is what one cannot use" (1066–67),[32] and "What one does not use is a heavy burden" (684),[33] clearly seems intended to contrast the present state of his scientific research with one in which it would be possible to know what is useful and to use what is knowable.[34] Faust addresses these words to Wagner in Part One, and it becomes a hilariously bitter caricature of Faust's quest for a usable natural science that Wagner—apparently with the help of Mephistopheles (6684–85, 6990)—should turn out in Part Two to have been able to create the Homunculus in his laboratory.[35] Creating human life is something that Faust the master and alchemist has never been able to accomplish.[36] As Wagner, who obviously does not share his master's reawakened sexual ardor, explains about traditional methods of human procreation, "The old-fashioned method of procreating we now call sheer nonsense.

29. Hier ist es Zeit, durch Taten zu beweisen, / Daß Manneswürde nicht der Götterhöhe weicht.

30. Dieser Erdenkreis / Gewährt noch Raum zu großen Taten.

31. Weisinger 1988, 31–32.

32. Was man nicht weiß, das eben brauchte man, / Und was man weiß, kann man nicht brauchen.

33. Was man nicht nützt, ist eine schwere Last.

34. Hahn 1979, 243–57.

35. Enders 1948, 76–117; Strich 1949, 84–116.

36. Gray 1952, 205–20, analyzes the relation of the Homunculus to alchemy.

That tender spot from which life sprang, that gracious inner force pushing outward and taking and giving, defining its own identity by appropriating first what is near, then what is remote—this has now been deposed from its privileged position" (6838–44).[37] With the demythologizing of all that mystery—which would presumably encompass even Faust's divine "Queen" (9191) and adored "Goddess" (6510, 9949), Helen of Troy—all that is left, Wagner explains fatuously, is: "What once was exalted as 'the mysterious quality' in Nature, that we dare to attempt with our own intelligence; and what she used to organize, that we now allow to crystallize" (6857–60).[38] This is an ultimate burlesque of the rationalistic philosophy and reductionistic natural science of the Enlightenment, made all the more ironic when the Homunculus, Wagner's "offspring, shows itself immediately to be capable of love" and goes off in search of a mate.[39]

But the utilitarian quest also carries over into Part Two in an even more substantive way, when it leads Faust to his greatest scientific triumph, which is also his greatest technological triumph, the reclamation of land from the sea. Invoking the aid of Mephistopheles with the words, "That is my wish, a risk that I want you to help me take!"[40] he describes it: "Thereupon I said to myself, as I hurriedly laid one plan after another: 'Have some delightful fun, by blocking the imperious sea from the shore, setting boundaries to its watery expanse and forcing it to turn back upon itself'" (10227–33).[41] As "delightful fun," the vast engineering project carries out another of the distinctions and definitions formulated by Goethe in his *Maxims and Reflections*: "Governing and having fun do not go

37. Wie sonst das Zeugen Mode war, / Erklären wir für eitel Possen. / Der zarte Punkt, aus dem das Leben sprang, / Die holde Kraft, die aus dem Innern drang / Und nahm und gab, bestimmt sich selbst zu zeichnen, / Erst Nächstes, dann sich Fremdes anzeignen, / Die ist von ihrer Würde nun entsetzt.

38. Was man an der Natur Geheimnisvolles pries, / Das wagen wir verständig zu probieren, / Und was sie sonst organisieren ließ, / Das lassen wir kristallisieren.

39. Parkes-Perret 1984, 249.

40. Das ist mein Wunsch, den wage zu befördern!

41. Da faßt' ich schnell im Geiste Plan auf Plan: / Erlange dir das köstliche Genießen, / Das herrische Meer vom Ufer auszuschließen, / Der feuchten Breite Grenzen zu verengen / Und, weit hinein, sie in sich selbst zu drängen.

together. Having fun means to belong to oneself and to others in happiness; governing means to be of benefit to oneself and to others with an earnest sense of purpose."[42] For according to Faust, it is "a great error" to suppose (as Mephistopheles summarizes the beliefs of the young Emperor) "that there can be a desirable and lovely compatibility between governing and having fun at the same time, and that it can work" (10249–52). Faust himself is under no such idealistic delusion, and he never has been. It is part of his skeptical credo, in the opening soliloquy of the drama, to admit that he has lost not only all joy in his scientific work, as well as any expectation that it can lead him to truth, but also any notion that through his science he could be, as Goethe put it in his *Maxims and Reflections,* "of benefit to oneself and to others with an earnest sense of purpose." No, none of that is possible any longer for Faust, because "Faust has already put behind him the purely theoretical path to the totality of things."[43] He has therefore lost his taste for both teaching and learning. "I have been deprived of all pleasure in my work," he admits. "I do not imagine that I can know anything properly, nor do I imagine that I can teach others anything that will improve and convert them" (370–73). Wagner seeks to carry this position to its logical conclusion when, in a chilling anticipation of rationalizations voiced just over a century after Goethe's death,[44] he responds to Faust's account of how he had poisoned all those thousands of people in the name of medical science, by assuring his master that it is enough for "a man of integrity . . . if you advance the progress of science" (1057, 1062), regardless of the human and moral consequences of the outcome.

Even being well-liked cannot provide Faust with any lasting sense of fulfillment. He has heard Wagner gush, in a mixture of admiration and envy, "What gratification a great man like you must get from the adulation of the multitude! How fortunate a man is if he can use his talents to gain such an advantage!" (1011– 14). This is no "advantage" at all for Faust; and so, when Mephis-

42. *Maximen und Reflexionen,* #966.
43. Balthasar 1947, 486.
44. Katz 1972, 292–306.

topheles describes his own yearning for such adulation by the "human ant heaps," so that "wherever I would go, driving or on horseback, I would always be the center of attraction, the object of reverence for hundreds of thousands of people" (10151–54), that simply adds fuel to Faust's alienation. "That can never satisfy me," he explains. "One can take pleasure in watching the common people thriving and living well according to their own tastes, and even studying and getting an education. But all one accomplishes is to raise up a generation of rebels" (10155–59). For neither the physical well-being of the common people nor their intellectual and spiritual improvement brings him—or them, for that matter —any lasting satisfaction, and they turn into "rebels." Yet he retains his ambition, his "power for bold action," not for fame, nor even any longer for carnal pleasure, but for "authority and power! The deed is everything, fame is nothing" (10184–88). When Mephistopheles nevertheless reminds him of his prospects for fame and for "poets who will celebrate your brilliance to posterity and will use nonsense to advance the cause of still more nonsense" (10189–91),[45] that is, of course, another of Goethe's seriously in-tended jests about the "nonsense" in the composition of his own poetic work, *Faust.*

Although Doctor Faust the polymath is—as was Goethe the polymath—a man of "a hundred scholarly disciplines" (657) also as a natural scientist, there are clearly some disciplines of scientific and technological research in which he—and, not surprisingly, Goethe—has a special interest from the very beginning and in which he remains interested throughout his life and throughout his association with Mephistopheles.[46] Therefore they are also espe-cially relevant to the study of Faust as theologian. These pertain both to the physical and biological sciences, especially medicine. Three of Faust's most dithyrambic celebrations of physical Nature, all in Act IV of Part Two, are also surprisingly detailed scientific

45. Doch werden sich Poeten finden, / Der Nachwelt deinen Glanz zu künden, / Durch Torheit Torheit zu entzünden.

46. Henel 1949, 507–32, is a succinct and useful general summary; Müllner 1935 and Loesche 1944 draw specific connections between the scientific treatises and *Faust.*

dissertations. Each of these, and especially the second, plays a significant part in the articulation of Faust's pantheism, but they deserve to be cataloged first for their science. A geological essay is the first of them.[47] It begins with the personal statement: "To me, massive mountains may be noble, but they remain mute, so that I do not ask where they came from nor why they should exist." Nevertheless, Faust admits to being fascinated by the processes of geological evolution, which are a special manifestation of Nature: "When Nature had established herself upon her own foundations, she neatly rounded off the globe of the Earth, finding enjoyment in peaks and canyons, lining up rock on rock and hill on hill, and then bringing the slopes of the foothills, gently and softly, into the valleys" (10095–10105).[48]

The discussion and guided tour take Faust and Mephistopheles next to a consideration of oceanography.[49] Faust opens with a description of his experience of the sea: "My eye was drawn to the vast sea. It swelled up in order to raise itself up as a tower, and then it relented, spilling its waves to ravage the breadth of the flat beach with a storm" (10198–10201).[50] But then he admits that his reverence before the awesome power of Nature as revealed in the power of the sea clashed with his conviction that "what one does not use is a heavy burden," as he had said in an earlier context (684). It seemed an inexcusable waste, "and that irritated me. The freedom of the spirit, which cherishes the rights of others, is deeply disturbed at such arrogance asserting itself immoderately, violently"

47. Magnus 1949, 200–221, and Wells 1965, 92–137, deal with Goethe as geologist.

48. Gebirgesmasse bleibt mir edel-stumm, / Ich frage nicht woher und nicht warum. / Als die Natur sich in sich selbst gegründet, / Da hat sie rein den Erdball abgeründet, / Der Gipfel sich, der Schluchten sich erfreut / Und Fels an Fels und Berg an Berg gereiht, / Die Hügel dann bequem hinabgebildet, / Mit sanftem Zug sie in das Tal gemildet.

Emrich 1957, 374–78, comments on this speech.

49. Hohlfeld 1936, 275–82, indicates some possible historical backgrounds for this.

50. Mein Auge war aufs hohe Meer gezogen; / Es schwoll empor, sich in sich selbst zu türmen, / Dann ließ es nach und schüttete die Wogen, / Des flachen Ufers Breite zu bestürmen.

(10202–5).[51] As it stood, the sea operated on the principle of being "sterile itself and sharing its sterility with others" (10213). Although it showed "wave after wave, seething with power," the net result of all that "power" was nil: "Nothing has been accomplished" (10216–17). Because "the endless cycle of tides now replaces the trajectory of despair in representing the endless cycle of the mind by which all our creative energy always brings us back to where we started,"[52] the combination of "irritation [Verdruß]" and "despair [Verzweiflung]" that Faust the natural scientist expresses here eventually plays its part in the transition to the denouement of the drama, and thus to morality and monotheism.[53]

The third of these scientific discourses is especially interesting because of its echoes of Goethe's *Theory of Colors*, which despite its title is a treatise on optics as a whole and not only on color.[54] Indeed, a recent study has shown it to be even more than that, by drawing provocative lines of connection between Goethe's *Theory of Colors* and his theological thought, with special implications also for the ideas being analyzed here.[55] Faust presents a meticulous analysis of the optical phenomenon known as Fata Morgana, but it is occasioned by military maneuvers. Observing the battle, the Emperor is puzzled by what he sees; and, probably because of his deepening entanglement with the sorcery of Faust and Mephistopheles, of which he eventually repents (11003),[56] he concludes, somewhat hastily: "What is happening is not in accordance with Nature." But Faust the natural scientist knows that it actually is in accordance with Nature, and he reminds the Emperor: "Have you never heard about the mists that arise on the Sicilian coast? There, in broad daylight, a strange sight appears in mid-air, surrounded by

51. Und das verdroß mich; wie der Übermut / Den freien Geist, der alle Rechte schätzt, / Durch leidenschaftlich aufgeregtes Blut / Ins Mißbehagen des Gefühls versetzt.

52. Bennett 1986, 190.

53. K. Lohmeyer 1927, 123–27.

54. Matthaei 1947, 59–148, catalogs this and other echoes from this treatise in the drama; on its controversy with Newton, see Sepper 1988 and, in brief, Duck 1988, 512–14.

55. Schöne 1987.

56. Wittkowski 1968, 141–44, reads it differently.

its own peculiar haze: cities shift to and fro, gardens rise and fall, as one image after another tumbles through the air" (10584–92). This is, then, only a mirage, not the result of demonic and supernatural powers; these powers have, nevertheless, been operative in various other ways during the battle, ways that the devil tries to pass off as "the cunning practiced in war to win battles," but that are, as Faust recognizes and admits, "Lies! The deception of witchcraft! Sheer trickery!" (10300–10301).

Another field of natural science that Faust studies is medicine,[57] one of the four major faculties in which Doctor Faust has, according to his opening words, "with strain and sweat studied [his] way all through" (354–57). Even before enrolling in the university he participated actively in the practice of his physician father, for which the father is undeservedly remembered by the peasant population with a profound gratitude that is tinged with critical irony: "Many a person is standing here alive whom your father snatched from the fever when he put an end to the pestilence." The son, too, deserves some of the credit (or blame); for, the old peasant continues, "As a young man at the time you went into each house where someone was sick. Many corpses were carried out, but you came out alive and well. You withstood many difficult crises. You helped us, and the Helper above helped you." But Faust picks up on the peasant's closing words, to divert the credit (or blame) to God: "Bow down to the One above, who teaches us to help and who sends help" (997–1010). For he is well aware, as he says a little later to Wagner, "how little father and son deserved this reputation!" (1032–33).

The science in which father and son were both engaged was alchemy.[58] It was put into the service of medicine, and with disastrous consequences. As Faust confesses, "With our infernal drugs we did more harm in these hills and valleys than the plague did. I myself administered the poison to thousands, who faded away." But the response was, he adds, that "it had to be my experience that they praised their heartless murderers" (1050–55), which may

57. Nager 1990.
58. Gray 1952 is an illuminating discussion.

help to explain why he has given up on any expectation that his science can be of benefit to humanity (370–73). In this as in other respects, the cynical advice dispensed to the entering student by Mephistopheles dressed in Faust's academic garb speaks also for Faust, or at any rate for part of him, in the devastating satire of medical tricks of the trade beginning with the words: "The essence of medicine is easy to grasp: you study your way all through the macrocosm and the microcosm—and then you have to let things happen the way God pleases." This is followed by a description of various techniques such as the taking of the pulse "with sly and ardent glances" (2011–36). Yet even on Classical Walpurgis Night, the medical preoccupation continues, being borne now by Chiron (Cheiron), a centaur renowned for his medical knowledge and skill.[59] Faust salutes him, not only as "the great man, the noble pedagogue, who became famous for educating a nation of heroes" (7337–38),[60] but specifically as the celebrated physician of Classical antiquity, "the physician who names every plant and who knows every root, who brings healing to the sick and relief to the wounded. Him I embrace here with all the power of spirit and body!" (7345–48).[61] One ground for his admiration of Chiron would seem to be that very contrast between ordinary physicians and this exceptional man, of whom the Sphinx said: "If he makes himself available to you, you will have come a long way" (7201).

The relation of Faust's natural science to his pantheistic philosophy and theology makes itself clear also in his use of the ancient symbols of the macrocosm and the microcosm (at 429), to which Mephistopheles alludes in the ironic advice about medicine just quoted (2012). Because "Goethe imbeds the psychological play of Faust in a cosmic drama,"[62] Faust seems always to be relating his empirical investigation of Nature to his inquiry into its inner being.

59. Jakob Escher-Bürkli in Pauly-Wissowa 1893–1963, 3:2302–8.

60. Der große Mann, der edle Pädagog, / Der, sich zum Ruhm, ein Heldenvolk erzog.

61. Den Arzt, der jede Pflanze nennt, / Die Wurzeln bis ins tiefste kennt, / Dem Kranken Heil, dem Wunden Linderung schafft, / Umarm' ich hier in Geist- und Körperkraft!

62. Roos 1952, 40.

In his study-laboratory at the very beginning of the drama, Faust contrasts "living Nature" with the "bones and skeletons" that surround him (414–17), the obvious implication being that Nature, as "living Nature," is the ultimate object of his pursuit even when he is engaged in the empirical investigation of skeletal remains. And conversely, he seems always to relate his language about God to this *Naturphilosophie.*[63] That becomes explicit above all in the nearest thing to a credo anywhere in the drama, with its echoes of various theological sources, including the discourses of Gregory of Nyssa on the namelessness of God.[64] The credo is delivered in response to Margarete's cross-examination—or "catechizing," as Mephistopheles calls it contemptuously (3523)—in her questions, "Now tell me, what is your stand on religion?" (3415) and again, "Do you believe in God?" (3426) and yet again, "So you do not believe?" (3430). To all of this Faust replies with his own confession of faith, which is, as has been said of Goethe's faith, "a wholly, even obsessively, personal piety, *his* relation with *his* heavenly Father, and no one else's":[65] "Who can dare to name him? Who can dare to make the confession: 'I believe in him'? Who can be sensitive and yet presume to say: 'I do not believe in him'? All-embracing, All-preserving, does he not grasp and preserve you and me and himself? Is that not the Heaven vaulting there above? Does not Earth lie solidly beneath us? And are not the eternal stars looking at us in a friendly way as they rise above us?" (3432–45).[66]

The naïveté of Margarete's reaction to all of this, "That is all well and good. The pastor says approximately the same thing, though with somewhat different words" (3459–61), does not obscure the chasm between the orthodox Christian doctrine of contin-

63. Jockers 1957, 90–147.

64. Elizabeth M. Wilkinson in Reiss 1972, 242–58; Gregory's doctrine of the namelessness of God is discussed in Pelikan 1993, 209–14.

65. Boyle 1991, 1:191.

66. Wer darf ihn nennen? / Und wer bekennen: / Ich glaub' ihn. / Wer empfinden, / Und sich unterwinden / Zu sagen: ich glaub' ihn nicht? / Der Allumfasser, / Der Allerhalter, / Faßt und erhält er nicht / Dich, mich, sich selbst? / Wölbt sich der Himmel nicht dadroben? / Liegt die Erde nicht hierunten fest? / Und steigen freundlich blickend / Ewige Sterne nicht herauf? Melzer 1932, 163–72, comments on this entire scene.

gent creation and this pantheistic confession, which sheds "the most powerful light on his world view."[67] For Faust, Nature had not come into being as the contingent product of the sovereign act of a transcendent Creator, as Judeo-Christian orthodoxy contended, but "had established herself upon her own foundations" (10097).[68] Even the pompous Chancellor discerns the difference when he denounces the devil's use of such terms as "Nature" and "Spirit" as "atheism" and "heresy" (4897–99). But this credo is only the most well-rounded of Faust's many statements of the pantheistic faith. The magisterial work on the intellectual history of the age of Goethe has spoken of a "a thoroughgoing pantheism" whose "most magnificent representation . . . must necessarily be the Faust poem."[69] Yet a theological critic has argued against "putting the various religious positions—pantheism, polytheism, and monotheism—on the same level," and has attempted to substitute the more precise technical term *panentheism* as "the real thematic center" in Goethe; despite his arguments for this, however, he also must acknowledge that Goethe "repeatedly seems to employ the concept 'pantheism' quite without self-consciousness."[70] This is, then, at the very least a faith that is imbued with "tendencies that clearly move in the direction of pantheism."[71] To a considerable extent, the historical question of Goethe's "pantheism" is tied to the question of his relation to Spinoza, and thus to the appropriateness of "pantheism" as a term for Spinoza's doctrine of God.[72] For our narrower purposes here, the term would seem to be an accurate one to use for Faust's system—and, in the judgment of several scholars, even for Goethe's.[73]

In his opening monologue, as he contemplates the symbol of the macrocosm, Faust is moved to a pantheistic rhapsody, which is identical with a monologue in *Urfaust* (94–100): "How everything

67. Burger 1963, 151.
68. "Deus sive Natura," Möbus 1964, 176–88.
69. Korff 1966, 520; also Jarras 1969, 28.
70. Thielicke 1982, 55–59, 100–101n.
71. Richard Brinkmann in Dürr and Molnár 1976, 179.
72. Boyle 1991, 1:282–85.
73. Biese 1893, 3–25, Hoffmann 1932–33, 1–14, and Dilthey 1964, 394–97.

is weaving itself into a totality, one thing active and alive in another! How the heavenly powers ascend and descend, passing the golden vessels to one another, coursing from Heaven to Earth on wings of blessed fragrance, with all resounding harmoniously through the All!" (447–53).[74] Therefore the Easter message of victory over death and original sin through the resurrection of Christ—as the Choir of the Angels intones, "Christ is risen! Joy to mortal man, who was entangled in woes that were destructive, insidious, and hereditary" (737–41),[75] a message with which he is, as he says, "familiar since my youth"—has in fact, ever since his youth, usually awakened in him not the Easter faith of orthodox Christianity but a pantheistic nature mysticism: "An incomprehensibly lovely yearning drove me to go out through woods and meadows, and amid a thousand ardent tears I sensed a new world arising for me. This song heralded the merry games of childhood and the free happiness of the celebration of spring" (769–80).[76] The very names "Easter" in English and "Ostern" in German indicate that this "celebration of spring" has long been linked in uneasy tension with the Christian Easter, as it was already with the Jewish Passover; but for Faust it seems to have absorbed them.

Many apologists for Christianity have taken a miracle as a basis for faith; thus Mephistopheles, having produced wine from the wood of a table, sardonically paraphrases the preacher's appeal for a *sacrificium intellectus:* "The wooden table can produce wine, too. This is a profound insight into Nature! This is a miracle, only believe!" (2287–89). But even in response to the most sublime

74. Wie alles sich zum Ganzen webt, / Eins in dem andern wirkt und lebt! / Wie Himmelskräfte auf und nieder steigen / Und sich die goldnen Eimer reichen! / Mit segenduftenden Schwingen / Vom Himmel durch die Erde dringen, / Harmonisch all das All durchklingen!

75. Christ ist erstanden! / Freude dem Sterblichen, / Den die verderblichen, / Schleichenden, erblichen / Mängel umwanden.

76. Ein unbegreiflich holdes Sehnen / Trieb mich, durch Wald und Wiesen hinzugehn, / Und unter tausend heißen Tränen / Fühlt' ich mir eine Welt entstehn. / Dies Lied verkündete der Jugend muntre Spiele, / Der Frühlingsfeier freies Glück.

Kühnemann 1938 expounds the relation of Faust to the "Ostergedanke."

miracle of all, the resurrection of Jesus Christ from the dead, Faust reverses that polarity, making faith the basis of miracle and declaring: "I hear the message all right, but what I lack is the faith, the faith of which a miracle is the dearest child. I do not dare to strive to reach the spheres from which this lovely message resounds" (765–68).[77] Even now, consequently, the "heavenly tones" of the Easter message do not raise Faust to heaven, where, as the Choir of the Disciples proclaims, "The One who was buried, now living and exalted, has gloriously ascended" (785–88). Instead they restore him to Earth from the brink of suicide: "O sound forth, you sweet tones of heaven! There is a tear in my eye, and I belong to the Earth again!" (783–84). For it is Earth, or more precisely Earth as part of the All of Nature, that is the object of his reverence, not the Heaven of the church's Easter faith.[78]

Just as the Easter message provokes that pantheistic reverence in Faust, so, too, does his love for Margarete. With the help of Mephistopheles, he has obtained access to her room just after she has left it, and he exclaims, as would any young lover: "O beloved hand! So godlike! Through you this cottage is changed into a kingdom of heaven." But he continues: "O Nature! Here, in delicate dreams, you shaped the inborn angel in her!" (2707–12). By that conjunction of eroticism and nature mysticism, according to which the beloved is Nature's creature, Faust's pantheistic confession of faith in "the All-embracing, All-preserving" (3438–39) is able to move, without missing a beat, to his romantic love as yet another proof for the existence of God, or at any rate for this conception of God: "Am I not looking at you eye to eye? Does not All press in upon your head and heart, weaving its eternal mystery, invisibly-visibly near you? Fill your heart with that, be it ever so great, and when you have found complete bliss in feeling, why, then call it what you like: Call it happiness! Heart! Love! God! I

---

77. Die Botschaft hör' ich wohl, allein mir fehlt der Glaube; / Das Wunder ist des Glaubens liebstes Kind. / Zu jenen Sphären wag' ich nicht zu streben, / Woher die holde Nachricht tönt.

78. Requadt 1972, 87–91.

have no name for it. Feeling is all. A name is nothing but sound and smoke, obscuring the clear glow of Heaven" (3446–58).[79]

The editor of *Faust* has commented on this outburst: "Faust's pantheistic confession of faith proceeds above all from the greatness of Nature and the experience of the Infinite in the finitude of a beautiful and beloved human being, as well as from the inner feeling of dependence and of belonging to a sublime order of things. There is no mention here of the moral sense of obligation, upon which Goethe later places such emphasis."[80]

Faust's reverence for Nature, if not his pantheistic version of that reverence, is shared by others. One of its most naïve and charming expressions is the aria of Lynkeus as he is keeping watch:[81] "Born to see, appointed to keep watch, pledged to the tower, I am pleased with the world. I stare into the distance; at the near distance I see the moon and the stars, see the forest and the roe deer. Thus I see in all of them their eternal beauty. And as I find it pleasing, I find myself pleasing, too. You fortunate eyes, for what you have seen: be it what it may, it was so beautiful!" (11288–11303).[82]

Nevertheless, as has been pointed out by several scholars,[83] the reverence for Nature receives its most exalted articulation anywhere in *Faust* neither in the monologue of Lynkeus nor in any of Faust's own monologues but at the opening of the Prologue in Heaven, in the words of the Archangel Raphael (247–50), which

79. Schau' ich nicht Aug' in Auge dir, / Und drängt nicht alles / Nach Haupt und Herzen dir, / Und webt in ewigem Geheimnis / Unsichtbar sichtbar neben dir? / Erfüll davon dein Herz, so groß es ist, / Und wenn du ganz in dem Gefühle selig bist, / Nenn es dann, wie du willst, / Nenn's Glück! Herz! Liebe! Gott! / Ich habe keinen Namen / Dafür! Gefühl ist alles; / Name ist Schall und Rauch, / Umnebelnd Himmelsglut.

80. Trunz 1968, 522.

81. Harvey 1937, 252.

82. Zum Sehen geboren, / Zum Schauen bestellt, / Dem Turme geschworen, / Gefällt mir die Welt. / Ich blick' in die Ferne, / Ich seh' in der Näh' / Den Mond und die Sterne, / Den Wald und das Reh. / So seh' ich in allen / Die ewige Zier, / Und wie mir's gefallen, / Gefall' ich auch mir. / Ihr glücklichen Augen, / Was je ihr gesehn, / Es sei wie es wolle, / Es war doch so schön!

83. Wattenberg 1969, 67; also the biographical observations in Eppelsheimer 1982, 62–63.

are then echoed in the hymn of all three Archangels: "The very sight of it gives strength to the angels, because thou art unfathomable, and all thy sublime works are as glorious as they were on the first day" (267–70).[84] Yet the reverence for Nature receives its most plaintive articulation in the words of Faust himself a little later in the drama, a cry heard already in *Urfaust* (102–6): "Infinite Nature, where can I take hold of thee? You breasts, where are you? You fountains of all life, to which Heaven and Earth cling, to which this withered breast presses—you flow, you satisfy thirst, and am I to go on pining this way in vain?" (455–59).[85] Here infinite Nature has become the eternal Mother at whose breasts even Heaven and Earth themselves are nourished. In the Classical Walpurgis Night, the pygmies say that "in the East as in the West, Mother Earth delights in giving life" (7620–21), thus picking up on the same maternal metaphor for the Earth to which Faust has just alluded when he called himself the son of Gaia, Mother Earth.[86] He is, he says, "Antaeus," who needs to touch the Earth periodically to return to life (7077).[87]

But if "You breasts, where are you?" Faust's cry to the divine but absent Mother, is the most plaintive expression of his pantheism, another invocation of the maternal metaphor by Faust is the most puzzling and, in the opinion of most if not of all interpreters, the most profound.[88] It occurs in Act I of Part Two, where Faust exclaims: "The Mothers! Mothers! It has such an eerie sound!" (6217).[89] As the editor of the most commonly used English transla-

84. Der Anblick gibt den Engeln Stärke, / Da keiner dich ergründen mag, / Und alle deine hohen Werke / Sind herrlich wie am ersten Tag.

85. Wo fass' ich dich, unendliche Natur? / Euch Brüste, wo? Ihr Quellen alles Lebens, / An denen Himmel und Erde hängt, / Dahin die welke Brust sich drängt— / Ihr quellt, ihr tränkt, und schmacht' ich so vergebens? Observations on this in Wilkinson and Willoughby 1962, 102–3.

86. Samson Eitrem in Pauly-Wissowa 1893–1963, 7:467–80.

87. Konrad Wernicke in Pauly-Wissowa 1893–1963, 1:2339–43.

88. Enders 1948, 20–22, provides a convenient chronological summary of its evolution in Goethe's authorship.

89. Die Mütter! Mütter!—'s klingt so wunderlich! There is an extensive exegesis of this passage ascribed to Goethe in Eckermann, *Gespräche mit Goethe*, Part Two, 10 January 1830 (Bergemann 1987, 359–61).

tion of *Faust* has observed, "critics and scholars have been struck with a ponderous awe" in interpreting this scene.[90] Another commentator, with an especially sensitive ear for the language and meter of the poem, has described its mood as "one of being seized by the mystery in its incomprehensible greatness, fearfulness, and enchantment—and all of these at the same time."[91] And yet another is certainly correct in his rejection of the simplistic notion that "the name of the goddesses is a reminder to Faust of Gretchen, who became a mother through him, and that is why he shudders."[92]

These Mothers are identified by Mephistopheles as "goddesses," to whom he issues the appeal, "O Mothers, Mothers! Do let go of Faust!" (6366), and to whom Faust, upon finding Helen, cries out, "You Mothers! Mothers! This you must grant me!" (6558). A superficial reading of the myth on the basis of these passages would conclude that these "Mothers" who are "goddesses" pertain, in the Goethean typology being adopted in this book, to "the poetic artist as polytheist" more than to "the natural scientist as pantheist." The Choir before the Palace of Menelas likewise seems to be intoning the maternal metaphor in a polytheistic rather than a pantheistic context when it appeals to "Rhea, the exalted Mother of all the gods" (8969–70). As the Mother of all the gods, the Mother also of Zeus himself, however, Rhea does seem to transcend the pantheon of polytheism; in antiquity she was sometimes equated with Kybele.[93] Yet the title "goddesses" applied by Mephistopheles to these "Mothers" is qualified by his stipulation that they are "unknown to you mortals, and not a favorite subject of conversation among us either" (6218–19), a numinous quality that does not apply to most of the deities of polytheism, if to any of them. Although one interpreter sees here "a borrowed tone for the purpose of parody" and "a joking pseudo-myth, through which Mephistopheles hypnotizes Faust,"[94] another has suggested that

90. Hamlin 1976, 328.
91. May 1962, 86.
92. Rickert 1932, 313.
93. Josephus Heckenbrach in Pauly-Wissowa 1893–1963, 1A:339–41.
94. Meyer 1970, 25–26.

"the entire scene of the Mothers is the most transcendental scene that Goethe ever attempted," not only in *Faust* but almost anywhere in his works.[95] For the path to the Mothers is described in an apophatic language that seems in its reverential and awestruck tones to anticipate the closing strophe of the drama: "All that is transitory is only a parable. Here the inadequate becomes an event. Here the indescribable is accomplished. The Eternal Feminine leads us upward" (12104–11).[96] The apophatic language in the exchange between Faust and Mephistopheles about the Mothers breathes more of the atmosphere of Faust's pantheism than of any polytheism: "Where does the way lead? There is no way! It goes into the untrodden, the untreadable; it is a way into the unpermitted, the impermissible" (6222–24).[97] With the stage direction "shuddering," Faust continues in those tones: "To the Mothers! It always hits me like a thunderbolt! What is this word that I cannot stand hearing?" (6265–66). And when Faust finally gets to address the Mothers, the numinous and apophatic atmosphere persists, as is indicated also by another stage direction, "in magnificent tones, solemnly": "In your name, O Mothers, enthroned in the Boundless, dwelling eternally alone, yet in company. The images of life, mobile but lifeless, encircle your head. All that once was, is in motion there in all its splendor, seeking to be made eternal. You all-powerful forces, you part them in two" (6427–33).[98] The terms employed by Faust, such as "in the Boundless" or "in all its splendor" or "all-powerful forces," together with the stage directions, "shuddering" and "in magnificent tones, solemnly," do not seem to fit the gods of polytheism as these appear in *Faust;* but they do carry the connotations of his pantheism more than those of his

95. Emrich 1957, 219–20.

96. Alles Vergängliche / Ist nur ein Gleichnis; / Das Unzulängliche, / Hier wird's Ereignis; / Das Unbeschreibliche, / Hier ist's getan; / Das Ewig-Weibliche / Zieht uns hinan.

97. Wohin der Weg? / Kein Weg! Ins Unbetretene, / Nicht zu Betretende; ein Weg ans Unerbetene, / Nicht zu Erbittende.

98. In eurem Namen, Mütter, die ihr thront / Im Grenzenlosen, ewig einsam wohnt, / Und doch gesellig. Euer Haupt umschweben / Des Lebens Bilder, regsam, ohne Leben. / Was einmal war, in allem Glanz und Schein, / Es regt sich dort; denn es will ewig sein. / Und ihr verteilt es, allgewaltige Mächte.

polytheism, together with some connotations of his alchemy.[99] This suggests that in his converse with these Mothers Faust is dealing not with this or that particular and individual deity of polytheism but with the theme of Nature as the All. It is, therefore, in the very midst of his discussion with Mephistopheles about the Mothers that Faust comes to his most explicit formulation of the antithesis between the nihilism of Mephistopheles and his own pantheism: "In this Nothing of yours I hope to find the All" (6255–56).[100] Such an interpretation of the Mothers would, as the closing chapter of this book will suggest, also contribute to the resolution of the drama, when, in the closing lines of the drama, "the Eternal Feminine" is called "Virgin, Mother, Queen, Goddess" (12102–3), with "Mother" representing Faust's scientific pantheism, while his poetic polytheism is represented by "Queen" and "Goddess," and his moralistic monotheism is denoted by "Virgin," the title for Mary that encompasses all of the others.

Yet it turns out to be one of the seriously intended jests and one of the most amusing parodies of Faust's pantheistic reverence for Nature when, in a conversation between Mephistopheles and the Homunculus whom Wagner has created, the Homunculus confides to the devil, "Let me tell you confidentially: I am on the trail of two philosophers. I listened to them and they kept saying 'Nature! Nature!' I do not want to lose track of them. They surely understand terrestrial reality, and eventually I shall probably learn from them where it would be smartest for me to turn next" (7835–41). Mephistopheles, whose attitude to Nature seems best expressed in his remark to Faust, "What do I care! Let Nature be as it may!" (10124), can only comment here: "That you should do on your own, for where ghosts have taken over, even the philosopher is welcome" (7842–44), which would include both Thales and Anaxagoras.[101] For as Mephistopheles observed about philosophers

99. Gray 1952, 200–204.
100. Nur immer zu! wir wollen es ergründen, / In deinem Nichts hoff' ich das All zu finden.
Analysis in Marotzki 1987, 142–48.
101. Magnus 1949, 210–12.

much earlier, speaking to Faust (but apparently recalling the fourteenth-century academic parable associated with the name of John Buridan), "I tell you: a rascal who engages in speculation is like an animal that is being led around and around by an evil spirit on a barren heath, while all the time there is lush green pasture near by" (1830–33).

But "the innermost spirits of nature and life" are "the Earth Spirit and the Mothers";[102] and in many ways the most intriguing articulation of Naturphilosophie in the entire drama, even by comparison with the Mothers, is the mythological figure of the Earth Spirit, which has been the object of intense scholarly investigation and controversy among Goethe specialists.[103] From that investigation some interpretive conclusions seem fairly clear: this figure is Goethe's invention, present already in *Urfaust* (107–60); it is identical neither with the person of God the Lord in the Prologue in Heaven nor with the person of Mephistopheles, though it bears some sort of relation to each,[104] even to the point of having been the power that changed the outward appearance of Mephistopheles into the form of the poodle;[105] and it acts decisively in determining the direction of Faust's development. Having experienced frustration as he contemplated the sign of the macrocosm in a book of pansophic speculation, he involuntarily turns the page of the book and discovers "the sign of the Earth Spirit," at which he cries out: "How different the effect this sign has upon me!" (460). What ensues is an interview between the Earth Spirit and the philosopher, which, it is important to note, takes place well before Mephistopheles has put in his appearance. From the outset Faust professes to sense a special affinity with the Earth Spirit, declaring: "You, Earth Spirit, are closer to me" (461). And again: "It is I, it is Faust, and I am the same as you!" (500). And yet again: "You busy spirit, flitting around the wide world, how near I feel myself to be to you!" (510–11). The Earth Spirit describes himself in language of a

102. E. Heller 1952, 44.
103. The nature of the question is well summarized in Mason 1959, 81–85.
104. Wehnert 1908, 758–68.
105. Mason 1960, 66–67.

decidedly pantheistic flavor: "In floods of life, in a storm of deeds, I seethe up and down, I weave back and forth! I am birth and the grave, an eternal sea, a fluctuating weaving, a glowing life. And so I am active at the whirring loom of time, and I fashion the living garment of the Godhead" (501–9).[106] It is in that activity of weaving Nature and Earth as "the living garment of the Godhead" that Faust the pantheist seeks to find his bond with the Earth Spirit. The Earth Spirit, however, neither reciprocates the superficial sense of affinity nor acknowledges Faust's claim to understand him, brushing him off with the harsh words, "You are equal only to the spirit that you can comprehend, not to me!" and vanishing (512–13).

But that is not the last word about the Earth Spirit. For much later in Part One it is apparently the Earth Spirit to whom Faust, in a powerful monologue "almost certainly written in 1788–9" in Italy,[107] pours out his heartfelt thanks for all the things he has received, including the love of Margarete, apparently through the dark powers of Mephistopheles:[108] "You sublime spirit, you gave me all I asked for, gave me everything." Specifically Faust thanks him for the fulfillment at last of his pantheistic yearnings, far transcending the cool objectivity of scientific observation: "You gave me glorious Nature as my kingdom, as well as the power to feel her and enjoy her. What you granted me was not a chilly and wondering visit, but the opportunity to gaze into her deep breast, as into the bosom of a friend."[109] As a result, he has now found the kinship with Earth and with all her inhabitants—and with her

106. In Lebensfluten, im Tatensturm / Wall' ich auf und ab, / Webe hin und her! / Geburt und Grab, / Ein ewiges Meer, / Ein wechselnd Weben, / Ein glühend Leben, / So schaff' ich am sausenden Webstuhl der Zeit / Und wirke der Gottheit lebendiges Kleid.

107. Boyle 1991, 1:629.

108. On the identification of this "Geist" and the "Erdgeist," the comments of Atkins 1953, 424–25; on this monologue, H. Jaeger 1949, 395–402; on its evolution in various recensions of the work, Mohr 1940, 181–83.

109. Gabst mir die herrliche Natur zum Königreich, / Kraft, sie zu fühlen, zu genießen. Nicht / Kalt staunenden Besuch erlaubst du nur, / Vergönnest mir, in ihre tiefe Brust, / Wie in den Busen eines Freundes, zu schauen.

Spranger 1946, 233–34, and Brenn 1981, 403A–406, are brief commentaries on these words.

four elements—that was shimmering before him at their initial encounter: "You let the succession of living things pass before me, and you teach me to know my brethren in the quiet heath, in the air, and in the water." But it is not only in serene contemplation that this oneness with Earth is revealed: "And when the storm rages and groans in the forest, shattering the giant pine, which, as it falls, crushes the neighboring growth and makes the hillside thunder back with hollow noise, then you guide me to the safety of a cave, you reveal me to myself, and mysterious and profound wonders manifest themselves to my own breast," until the knowledge of the All blends with the deeper knowledge of the self, or, to stay with the persistent echoes of the maternal metaphor, "the opportunity to gaze into her deep breast, as into the bosom of a friend," conveys the meaning of "my own breast" (3217–34). And therefore, in a prose paraphrase of this monologue, Faust can address the Earth Spirit as "thou great and glorious spirit, thou who hast deigned to appear before me, thou who dost know my heart and my soul."[110]

What characterizes Faust's "heart" and his "soul" in the pantheistic reflection on his kinship with Earth and Nature as divine Mother—as it also characterizes his polytheistic devotion as a poet to Helen, as well as his eventual monotheistic rediscovery of morality and salvation through Mary—is a profound sense of reverence.[111] As he tries (vainly) to explain to Mephistopheles, "The capacity for awe is the best feature of humanity. The world may extract a heavy payment for such feelings, but someone who has been stirred feels the Numinous profoundly" (6272–74). The vision of the setting sun, identified as a "goddess," arouses that sense of reverence and awe (1070–99). The pantheistic view of Nature, moreover, supplies the content of his view of human nature, specifically for his doctrine of the image of God. "I am the image of the Godhead!" he exclaims to the Earth Spirit (516). A little later he repeats that doctrine in fairly traditional terms: "I, the image of the Godhead, which soon thinks of itself as approaching the mirror of

110. *Faust*, Part One, "Trüber Tag" (Trunz 1968, 138, 11–13).
111. Franz 1932, 109–50, on "Ehrfurcht."

eternal truth, indulging in the clear light of Heaven and shuffling off my earthly origin." But he goes on to put the image of God into its proper context, that is for him, into its pantheistic context: "I, superior to the cherubim, as one whose free energy ominously dared to flow through the veins of Nature and, by creativity, to enjoy the very life of the gods" (614–21),[112] with Nature seen as the body of God through whose veins man, as the image of God, has the privilege of flowing.

That sense of reverence before the All has enabled him as a scientist, in his study of Nature, "to gaze into her deep breast, as into the bosom of a friend" (3223–24), and to address his worship to each of her phenomena in turn. Perhaps the most basic of these is, in keeping with the revealing activity of the Earth Spirit, Earth herself. Thus Mephistopheles admits to failure in his efforts to disrupt her continuity: "That which stands over against nothingness, this clumsy world—no matter what I have tried—waves, storms, earthquake, fire—I have not been able to get at it; and when it is all over, sea and land remain just as they were" (1363–68).[113] In response, Faust, punning on his own name, "Faust [fist]," affirms that continuity as an eternal and creative force against which Mephistopheles, as "the strange son of Chaos," wields his nihilistic power in vain: "Against the eternally active and benignly creative force, all you can put in opposition is that cold devil's fist of yours, which clenches itself malevolently but in vain!" (1379–84).[114] Later, Faust's apostrophe to Earth celebrates that eternally active and benignly creative force: "The pulses of life are beating, fresh and strong, in order to give a gentle greeting to this ethereal dawn. And thou, Earth, hast been steady through the night and art now breathing at my feet with new vitality. Thou art beginning to

112. Ich, mehr als Cherub, dessen freie Kraft / Schon durch die Adern der Natur zu fließen / Und, schaffend, Götterleben zu genießen / Sich ahnungsvoll vermaß . . .

113. Was sich dem Nichts entgegenstellt, / Das Etwas, diese plumpe Welt, / So viel als ich schon unternommen, / Ich wußte nicht ihr beizukommen, / Mit Wellen, Stürmen, Schütteln, Brand— / Geruhig bleibt am Ende Meer und Land!

114. So setzest du der ewig regen, / Der heilsam schaffenden Gewalt / Die kalte Teufelsfaust entgegen, / Die sich vergebens tückisch ballt!

surround me with the desire to go on striving for the highest level of existence" (4679–85).[115] To such contemplation of the divine creation, "a Paradise appears all around me" (4694), which is a model—perhaps one might even be justified to call it an "archetype"—of the human creation of "an image of Paradise" that he himself will eventually achieve (11086). And even in Act IV of Part Two, he still affirms a reverence before the mystery of a noble Earth with its massive mountains as a special product of Nature's creative activity: "When Nature had established herself upon her own foundations, she neatly rounded off the earthly sphere," which does not need the "extravagances" of human explanation and scientific speculation to achieve its fulfillment (10095–10104).

A comparison of these two passages suggests, however, that Earth exerts such a religious fascination over Faust above all not when she is geologically "noble but mute" but when she throbs with biological life and when "the pulses of life are beating, fresh and strong" in response to her, and when, therefore, "the savage mountain with all its chasms would not hinder my godlike flight" (1080–81).[116] That pulsing with life happens especially with the coming of spring, when, in the words of Faust's early paean, "The river and the brooks are set free from ice, through the gentle and quickening glance of spring; in the valley the joy of hope is turning green" (903–5).[117] It is clearly the spring, and not human subjectivity on its own, that originates this antiphonal response between Earth and the self, which even the black magic of Walpurgis Night on the eve of the first day of May cannot negate. As Faust and Mephistopheles enter on this adventure, Faust once more indites a

115. Des Lebens Pulse schlagen frisch lebendig, / Ätherische Dämmerung milde zu begrüßen; / Du, Erde, warst auch diese Nacht beständig / Und atmest neu erquickt zu meinen Füßen, / Beginnest schon, mit Lust mich zu umgeben, / ... Zum höchsten Dasein immerfort zu streben.

Türck 1921, 198–200, is a meditation on this passage.

116. As its title indicates, Salm 1971 is a fascinating exposition of "a biological view" of "the poem as plant"; Engard 1952 is a convenient collection and translation of Goethe's writings on botany, with a helpful historical introduction.

117. Vom Eise befreit sind Strom und Bäche / Durch des Frühlings holden, belebenden Blick; / Im Tale grünet Hoffnungsglück.

paean to spring: "To crawl through a labyrinth of valleys, and then to climb this boulder, from which the waterfall eternally splashes down—that is the pleasure that enhances such a journey! Spring is already weaving in the birch trees, and even the pines are beginning to feel it"—a "weaving" of the spring that recalls the weaving of Nature and Earth as "the living garment of the Godhead" by the Earth Spirit (501–9). And, in response, "Should it not have an effect also on our own limbs?" (3841–47). To open Part Two of the drama, Ariel, accompanied by Aeolian harps, echoes this celebration of the spring, in the name of all the children of Earth, including the nonhuman ones: "When the springtime shower of blossoms floats and sinks on all, and when the green blessing of the fields is twinkling at all the children of Earth, the host of little elf-spirits hurry to do what they can. We feel sorry for any unfortunate man, be he saint or sinner" (4613–20).[118]

Not only because water, along with Earth (and air and fire), is one of the four elements but because of its own numinous qualities, the sea is also an appropriate object of reverence. It is that for others than Faust, too, as when the Wanderer returns to the homestead of Philemon and Baucis, who had once rescued him from shipwreck (as, according to the account of Ovid's *Metamorphoses,* Philemon and Baucis extended their hospitality to Zeus and Hermes disguised as wanderers):[119] "Now let me step outside and gaze at the boundless sea. Let me kneel, let me pray. My breast is so deeply moved" (11075–78), only to be told by Philemon that Faust has, with the help of Mephistopheles and his sorcery, asserted dominion also over the sea, transforming its wild and destructive power into "an image of Paradise" (11082–11106).[120] Yet that transformation, accomplished as a consequence of Faust's demand to Mephistopheles to have his wish carried out (10233), is itself the outcome

118. Wenn der Blüten Frühlingsregen / Über alle schwebend sinkt, / Wenn der Felder grüner Segen / Allen Erdgebornen blinkt, / Kleiner Elfen Geistergröße / Eilet, wo sie helfen kann, / Ob er heilig, ob er böse, / Jammert sie der Unglücksmann.

119. Richard Wagner in Pauly-Wissowa 1893–1963, 3:153–54, citing Ovid *Metamorphoses* 8, 610–715.

120. This is expounded by Jantz 1978, 49–59.

of Faust's sense of awe before the might of the sea, as expressed in a passage of great descriptive power quoted earlier (10198–10201). In the eschatology of the drama, the technological outcome of this reverence for the sea contributes in turn, through the further maturing of Faust's character, to a moral outcome and to his eventual salvation. Or, to put it in the language of our fundamental typology, his pantheism as natural scientist leads to his monotheism as moral philosopher, but only by means of a dialectic with his polytheism as poetic artist.

CHAPTER THREE

The Poetic Artist as Polytheist

IN SPITE OF THE pantheistic-sounding language about the All that Faust the natural scientist employs—as when, in defending his religion to Margarete, he speaks of God as "the All-embracing, All-preserving" (3438–39), or when, in his introductory soliloquy, he describes how "all resounds harmoniously through the All" (453)—the term *pantheism* as such does not of course appear in the poem. The nearest *Faust* comes to the term is a scene in which the Chorus of Nymphs seems to pun on the Greek word *Pan* when it announces: "Here he comes! The All of the world is being set forth in the great god Pan" (5872–75).[1] For the word can refer either to the Greek god, "the great Pan" (in the masculine, as *ho Pan*), or to "the All of the world" (in the neuter, as *to Pan*).[2] It is a play on words going back to the Homeric hymns and to Plato,[3] but this passage, in a sense, puts polytheism into the service of pantheism. Because of the evolution of Goethe's *Faust*, especially with the composition and development of Part Two, this theme of polytheism becomes far more prominent in the final version of *Faust* than

1. Auch kommt er an! / Das All der Welt / Wird vorgestellt / Im großen Pan.

These lines are examined by D. Lohmeyer 1975, 100–104.

2. White 1980, 124.

3. Frank Brommer in Pauly-Wissowa 1893–1963, S 8:1005.

it was in *Urfaust.*[4] In addition to the many references throughout the drama to polytheism in relation to poetry and the other arts, there are at least three major sections in which Faust, under the tutelage of Mephistopheles as impresario, experiences polytheism in its depths: Walpurgis Night (3835–4222),[5] together with the ambiguous and problematic Walpurgis Night's Dream (4223–4398), which immediately follows it;[6] the Carnival (5065–5986);[7] and the Classical Walpurgis Night (7005–8487).[8] Walpurgis Night, the Witches' Sabbath, initiates Faust into some of the complexities of the demonic universe with which he has now entered into partnership, and that continues in the Walpurgis Night's Dream.[9] The night is filled with eerie beings: salamanders (3892), mice of many colors (3900–3901), and all such stuff as bad dreams are made on. In the final form of the drama Walpurgis Night has in some ways become a prelude to the Classical Walpurgis Night, poetically but also theologically one of the most ambitious and elaborate constructions of the entire work. But before the Classical Walpurgis Night can open, it is with the Carnival that the nexus of polytheist and poetic artist begins to become explicit, initiating the transition from the species of witchcraft (also polytheistic) represented by the original Nordic version of Walpurgis Night, to the poetic polytheism of Classical antiquity represented by the Classical Walpurgis Night, in which, as has been said, "everything that could serve as a reminder of ghostly apparitions is deliberately kept at a distance."[10]

That is the gradual process by which Faust the natural scientist becomes Faust the poetic artist as well, and eventually poet and

---

4. There is a chapter on Goethe's "interpretation of the history of religions" in Meinhold 1958, 113–71.

5. Materials on it are collected in the provocative essay "Walpurgisnacht," Schöne 1982, 107–230.

6. Hippe 1966, 67–75.

7. Inge Jensen in Holtzhauer and Zeller 1968, 165–77.

8. Schüpbach 1980 is a discussion especially of its theological significance; also helpful are: Atkins 1954, 64–78; Kohlschmidt 1955, 97–119; Rehder 1955, 591–611; and Reinhardt 1960, 309–56.

9. Jantz 1952, 359–408.

10. Petsch 1926a, 167.

priest in one.[11] For "his current role of magician-priest is an extension of that of showman-poet."[12] He is described in Part Two as "in priestly garb, crowned with a wreath, a miracle man, who now accomplishes the task he so confidently undertook. . . . He gets ready to bless the lofty work, and from now on there can only be good fortune" (6421–22, 6425–26).[13] Faust himself speaks of how his world has changed, now that he has found both Helen of Troy and his priestly vocation: "How pointless and confined the world was for me! What has it now become, since my priesthood? For the first time, desirable, deep-founded, permanent!" (6490–92).[14] Helen also becomes a test case of the difference between the time-bound scientific methodology of the scholar and the timeless aesthetic methodology of the poet, much to the disadvantage of science. Near the beginning of Classical Walpurgis Night, Faust, whose knowledge of Greek literature led Wagner to suppose upon overhearing one of his soliloquies that he was declaiming a Greek tragedy (522–25),[15] has just displayed his Classical erudition: the Sphinxes remind him of the tragedy of Oedipus, the Sirens of the epic of Odysseus (7185–86). But then Chiron, whom Faust consults on the advice of the Sphinxes as someone "running around on this night of spirits" who can assist him (7199–7201), sets Faust straight, in response to the repetition of the conventional wisdom of the scholars about the chronology of Helen's life: "I can see that the philologists have deceived you as well as themselves. There is something special about myth-born woman. The poet brings her into view as he needs to: she never grows up, never gets old, always

11. Boyle 1991, 1:633–41, has some informative comments on "poet" as a category for Goethe.
12. Atkins 1958, 138.
13. Im Priesterkleid, bekränzt, ein Wundermann, / Der nun vollbringt, was er getrost begann. . . . / Er rüstet sich, das hohe Werk zu segnen; / Es kann fortan nur Glückliches begegnen.
14. Wie war die Welt mir nichtig, unerschlossen! / Was ist sie nun seit meiner Priesterschaft? / Erst wünschenswert, gegründet, dauerhaft!
Boyle 1991, 1:523–29, comments on the relation between "the story of Faust and Helen" and "that of Faust and Gretchen"; Diener 1961 makes use of the concept of "archetype" to explain Helen.
15. Arens 1982, 98.

keeps her appetizing shape, is carried off in youth, and is still being courted in old age. Enough, the poet is not bound by chronology" (7426–33).[16]

Chiron possesses special unique qualifications to instruct Faust about many things, including the calling of the poet.[17] For he is, in Faust's words, "the great man, the noble pedagogue, who became famous for educating a race of heroes, the beautiful circle of the noble Argonauts, and all those who constructed the world of the poet" (7337–40),[18] in addition to being a famous physician.

By this emergence as poetic artist and priest, Faust fulfills the sacerdotal definition of the poet's service to "Sacred Poesy" (9863),[19] which acts as a theme for the drama from its beginning. Already in the Prelude on the Stage—which it does seem proper to read, in this respect at any rate, as a prelude to the drama as a whole[20]—that theme is sounded: "The poet is the only one who can work this miracle on so many different kinds of people. My friend, do it today!" (57–58).[21] It is that capacity to perform miracles for a variety of audiences that sets the poet apart from the vulgar crowd: "No, lead me rather to that quiet nook of Heaven's stillness, the only place where sheer joy blooms for the poet, where, with a divine hand, love and friendship create and nourish the

---

16. Ich seh', die Philologen, / Sie haben dich so wie sich selbst betrogen. / Ganz eigen ist's mit mythologischer Frau, / Der Dichter bringt sie, wie er's braucht, zur Schau: / Nie wird sie mündig, wird nicht alt, / Stets appetitlicher Gestalt, / Wird jung entführt, im Alter noch umfreit; / Gnug, den Poeten bindet keine Zeit.

The symbolism is examined in Emrich 1953, 58.

17. Classical material about "the significance of Chiron as, on the one hand, a physician and helpful friend and, on the other hand, an educator and teacher of knightly art" is conveniently assembled by Jakob Escher-Bürkli in Pauly-Wissowa 1893–1963, 3:2302–8.

18. Der große Mann, der edle Pädagog, / Der, sich zum Ruhm, ein Heldenvolk erzog, / Den schönen Kreis der edlen Argonauten / Und alle, die des Dichters Welt erbauten.

19. On the context of "Heilige Poesie," consult Elke Schümann-Heinke in Trunz and Loos 1971, 279–82, and Butler 1956, 197–208.

20. Seidlin 1949, 462–70.

21. Dies Wunder wirkt auf so verschiedne Leute / Der Dichter nur; mein Freund, o tu es heute!

blessings of the heart" (63–66).[22] Halfway through the drama, that celebration of the poet echoes yet again. The divine mission of the poet is defined in an address of Plutus (who is usually taken to be Faust) to the Boy Charioteer in the Carnival: "Only where you can look with a clear eye into that which is chaste and clear, be your own master and be confident only in yourself, where only the Good and the Beautiful are pleasing. Find solitude! That is the place to create a world of your own" (5693–96).[23] And the Boy Charioteer says of himself: "I am prodigality, I am Poesy; I am the poet, who finds completeness in squandering whatever is his very own" (5573–75).[24] The poet is seen here as, in the medieval phrase, simultaneously priest and sacrificial victim, spending himself and his substance in carrying out his service. This priestly vocation, according to the Prelude on the Stage, has a transcendent power to take control not only of the poet's audience but also of the poet himself, although the Director fails to see this when he says: "If you represent yourselves as poets, then deliver orders to Poesy" (220–21). The miracle of this vocation is specified in greater detail already there, and by means of a language of Classical polytheism that seems to anticipate the Classical Walpurgis Night of Part Two: "Who guarantees Olympus? Who brings the gods together? It is human power, revealed in the poet" (156–57).[25] The poetic composition of the drama is itself predicted by Mephistopheles to Faust, and then it is carried out, many centuries later, by Goethe and other poets, as the ironic words quoted earlier suggest (10189–91). In a

22. Nein, führe mich zur stillen Himmelsenge, / Wo nur dem Dichter reine Freude blüht, / Wo Lieb' und Freundschaft unsres Herzens Segen / Mit Götterhand erschaffen und erpflegen.

23. Nur wo du klar ins holde Klare schaust, / Dir angehörst und dir allein vertraust, / Dorthin, wo Schönes, Gutes nur gefällt, / Zur Einsamkeit!—Da schaffe deine Welt.

24. Bin die Verschwendung, bin die Poesie; / Bin der Poet, der sich vollendet, / Wenn er sein eigenst Gut verschwendet.

25. Wer sichert den Olymp? vereinet Götter? / Des Menschen Kraft, im Dichter offenbart.

These lines are the subject of comments by Girnus 1962, 1–32, and by Arens 1982, 40–41.

profound sense this "aesthetic apotheosis of man,"[26] the movement by which Faust, natural scientist and pantheist, becomes poetic artist and polytheist as well, may be said to set up the entire plot of the drama. It is noteworthy that in Faust's words, "The bold magician seeks out others; with openhanded generosity he enables all of them to see whatever miracles they wish" (6436–38), an earlier draft had "poet [Dichter]" rather than "magician [Magier]."[27]

In Goethe's version of Faust's existential crisis, his nostalgia for a lost youth and even his eroticism are in fact functions of a natural science and pantheism that have arrived at an intellectual, moral, and spiritual cul-de-sac.[28] That diagnosis of Faust's ailment is present from the very beginning. The books and scientific instruments with which Faust has surrounded himself as keys to the discovery of knowledge about Nature have led him instead to quite the opposite discovery, that "Nature, filled with mystery even in the light of day, will not let her veil be snatched away. What she does not will to reveal to your spirit, you will not be able to force out of her with bolts and levers" (672–75).[29] The veil of Nature remains impenetrable. When in his study, Faust acknowledges that he finds contentment in the glow of his desk lamp and in the exercise of his rational powers; but even here, as he says, "One yearns for the streams of life, oh, for the spring of life" (1194–1201). Therefore Faust confesses his sin of intellectual hubris: "I have puffed myself up too high. I belong only at your level. The sublime [Earth] Spirit has spurned me. Nature is closing herself to me" (1744–47). But note that he addresses this confession of sin, not to God with a plea for forgiveness as he should, but to Mephistopheles with an offer of a pact in exchange for aid in breaking out of his limitations. That confession, in turn, moves him to express

26. Möbus 1964, 203–4.

27. Die andern sucht der kühne Magier auf; / In reicher Spende läßt er, voll Vertrauen, / Was jeder wünscht, das Wunderwürdige schauen.

On the textual change, Hamlin 1976, 162 n. 3.

28. Kluge 1982.

29. Geheimnisvoll am lichten Tag / Läßt sich Natur des Schleiers nicht berauben, / Und was sie deinem Geist nicht offenbaren mag, / Das zwingst du ihr nicht ab mit Hebeln und mit Schrauben.

his dissatisfaction with the scholar's life as he has been leading it and, in what has been called "the sudden change from a striving for knowledge to a striving for pleasure, from the lodestar of the image of God to that of the image of man,"[30] to voice his yearning for the authenticity of sensuality and passion: "The web of thinking is torn to bits, and I have been nauseated at learning for a long time. Let us gratify our red-hot passions in the depths of sensuality!" (1748–51).[31] The sigh, "The web of thinking is torn to bits," is a paraphrase of Faust's opening words, describing his frustrating odyssey through all the branches of knowledge and science (354–64). But only in the total course of Faust's development does the depth of this alienation come fully into his consciousness, and into that of the reader. Goethe's original plan had been to dramatize that alienation, together with the relation of natural scientist and poetic artist, in a scene that would have parodied the doctoral disputation in the medieval university.[32]

It is the high skill of Mephistopheles, the "master of a thousand arts [Tausendkünstler],"[33] to exploit this alienation and satiety. For Faust's satiety is boredom, but it is more than boredom. Rather, it is, as he himself calls it, a "despair that was at the point of destroying my mind" (610–11),[34] a hopelessness based on the dichotomy that what is knowable is not useful and what is useful is not knowable (1064–67). In its symptoms and expression, therefore, Faust's predicament belongs to the classic sin of *acedia* in the catalog of vices developed by medieval monasticism, just as the arrogance of Mephistopheles is an echo of the corresponding monastic vice of *superbia*.[35] Mephistopheles is able to press his exploi-

30. Arens 1982, 189.

31. Des Denkens Faden ist zerrissen, / Mir ekelt lange vor allem Wissen. / Laß in den Tiefen der Sinnlichkeit / Uns glühende Leidenschaften stillen!

32. There is a rich and provocative discussion of this scene in Burdach 1926, 1–69.

33. The term appears, though without explicit identification of who is meant, in line 6072; but from Goethe's "sketch" of 1816 (Trunz 1968, 432) it is clear that he used it specifically for Mephistopheles.

34. Verzweiflung . . . , / Die mir die Sinne schon zerstören wollte.

35. Leonard Forster in Lange and Roloff 1971, 307–19.

tation of this satiety and hopelessness to the very limits agreed upon with the Almighty in the Prologue in Heaven (299–349). He ridicules the reclusive life of Faust the scientist and scholar: "Why should you be lurking there in caves and crevices, like a hoot owl?" (3272–73). The ridiculing of Faust as "owl" continues on Walpurgis Night, in words apparently spoken by Mephistopheles, "Hoot! Hoot owl! They are getting closer—screech owl, plover, and jay" (3889–90). For the owl is at one and the same time an ancient symbol of wisdom and an object of derision.

In the remarkable monologue he delivers while garbed in Faust's doctoral "cap and gown" (1846)—a monologue that did not appear in *Urfaust,* where Mephistopheles was garbed instead "in a nightgown, wearing a large periwig" (at 249)— Mephistopheles portrays Faust's contempt for rationality and science of every kind as a surefire path to sorcery and, through sorcery, to his own total domination over Doctor Faust. In the Prologue in Heaven he has already said to the Lord God about what Pascal called the grandeur and the misery of man: "He would be better off if you had not given him the glimmer of heavenly light. He calls it 'reason,' and all he uses it for is to become more beastly than any beast" (283–86). And now his announcement of the theme here, "a masterly summing up of Faust's character,"[36] at the same time provides a masterly summing up of the gradual unfolding of the plot, which employs but reworks the traditional theme of sorcery from the Faust legend:[37] "If you will only despise reason and science, the greatest of human powers, and let yourself be overpowered by the spirit of lies through deceit and sorcery—then I've already got you for sure" (1851–55).[38] "Reason and science," taken together, have "deceit and sorcery" as their demonic counterpart; for "the objectivity of theoretical outlook, which from the begin-

36. Steinhauer 1956, 190.
37. Hans Henning in Holtzhauer and Zeller 1968, 143–64.
38. Verachte nur Vernunft und Wissenschaft, / Des Menschen allerhöchste Kraft, / Laß nur in Blend- und Zauberwerken / Dich von dem Lügengeist bestärken, / So hab' ich dich schon unbedingt.
J. Müller 1980 is devoted to the "dramatic function" of this Mephistophelian monologue.

ning Faust believed he could leave totally behind him, suddenly acquires here a significance that elevates it far above existential magic."[39] In his opening soliloquy Faust has spoken of himself as "image of the Godhead, supposing myself to be very near to the reflection of eternal truth" (614–15).[40] Traditionally, whatever the original intention of the metaphor "image of God" in the Book of Genesis may have been, a Hellenized Christian theology has identified the content of the image as consisting chiefly in reason, free will, and immortality, each of these setting the human creature apart from the animals.[41] And when Faust, in the same soliloquy, goes on to speak of himself as "superior to the cherubim, as one whose free energy ominously dared to flow through the veins of Nature and, by creativity, to enjoy the very life of the gods" (618–21), this, in contrast, sets the human creature apart also from the holy angels, who, according to accepted teaching, share the rationality and the immortality of the image of God—though not in the same sense the free will, having been confirmed in holiness after the fall of Satan and his followers (as indeed saved humanity would be in heaven). But it is also in that soliloquy that Faust despairs both of rationality and of the image of God: "I do not resemble the gods! I can feel it only too well. I resemble the worm that crawls through the dust, feeding on the dust, and that is crushed to nothing and buried by the passing foot" (652–55).[42] He is now prepared, as Mephistopheles had hoped (1851–55), to "despise" the "reason [Vernunft]" of the image of God, just as he has also begun to despair of the "science [Wissenschaft]" of his scholarly vocation. Therefore, as part of his comprehensive renunciation, he pronounces a curse also upon reason and "upon the exalted opinion that the human spirit has of itself" (1591–92), and he tells Mephistopheles that he has a "breast which has been healed of the

39. Balthasar 1947, 497.

40. Ebenbild der Gottheit, das sich schon / Ganz nah gedünkt dem Spiegel ew'ger Wahrheit.

41. Pelikan 1993, 120–35.

42. Den Göttern gleich' ich nicht! Zu tief ist es gefühlt; / Dem Wurme gleich' ich, der den Staub durchwühlt, / Den, wie er sich im Staube nährend lebt, / Des Wandrers Tritt vernichtet und begräbt.

drive for knowledge" (1768). Yet the combination of "reason" as an inborn power with "science" as an acquired power is, according to the phrase employed by Mephistopheles in the present context, "the greatest of human powers." It may be a resonance of that phrase for Faust to say to Mephistopheles, upon hearing him refer to "the Mothers," that the sense of awe is the best thing there is about human nature (6272). This may in turn carry some reso- nance of his earlier exclamation: "A deep night, with ominous and sacred fear, awakens the better soul within us" (1179–81), a condi- tion that he goes on to specify as one in which "reason begins to speak again, and hope begins to bloom" (1198–99). It is that "better soul," in which a capacity for "hope" and for a reverent "awe" is joined with "reason," that Mephistopheles undertakes to overcome with "deceit and sorcery." The converse of this campaign would seem to be that the "deceit and sorcery" will not be over- come in turn, nor the power of Mephistopheles broken, until, in the "better soul" of Faust, "reason begins to speak again, and hope begins to bloom"—thus both reason and hope, but both of these in combination with the "faith" and the "loving grace" that Faust curses in his repudiation of all three cardinal Christian virtues (1604–6). That blossoming anew of hope, faith, and love, and in conjunction with Faust's reason, happens only at the drama's conclusion.

The deriding of traditional scholarship and science continues, in the scene that opens with the soliloquy of Mephistopheles about "reason and science," when, under the tutelage of Mephistopheles and in response to his leading questions, a young student, supposing the disguised Mephistopheles to be Faust, confesses to finding the life of the study and the library oppressive and unreal: "Inside these walls, these auditoriums, I can never be happy. It is such a con- stricted space, with no greenery, no trees; and in these lecture halls, on these benches, I lose the ability to hear or see or think" (1882–87).[43] The contempt for learning and science, together with the contrast between its deadly methodology and the living reality, can

43. In diesen Mauern, diesen Hallen / Will es mir keineswegs gefallen. / Es ist ein gar beschränkter Raum, / Man sieht nichts Grünes, keinen Baum, / Und in den Sälen auf den Bänken / Vergeht mir Hören, Sehn und Denken.

be sensed in the same scene, when Mephistopheles disguised as Faust describes in ironic tones what it is that scientists and scholars do: "If someone wants to understand and describe a living thing, the first step is to drive the spirit out of it. Then he has the parts in his hand, and the only thing that is missing is, alas, the spiritual bond!" (1936–39).[44] Escaping from life and reality, such pedantry has as its overriding intellectual ambition nothing short of "reducing and properly classifying all" (1944–45). Or, as Mephistopheles says much later about the life of learning: "I know it well, to be far along in years and still a student, in fact an old mossback! Even a man of learning goes on studying because there is nothing else he can do. One builds a modest house of cards, but even the greatest mind never completes it" (6637–41).[45] Those words appear in the Baccalaureus scene, when the young student returns. As he thinks about the figure whom he believes to be his old professor, he envisions him as a "living man who is like a corpse . . . and who dies of [the disease of] being alive" (6692–94). And then he greets him, in that full confidence that perennially seems to spring from belonging to a new generation: "If, old sir, the streams of Lethe have not yet engulfed your bald, bowed head, take a look and recognize your pupil, who has outgrown the academic drill. You seem to me to be the way you used to be; but as for me, I have become a different person" (6721–26).[46] Soon after that, the lampooning of pedantry reaches its climax in a scene that seems almost to be a burlesque of the Cinderella story. The Homunculus, whom Faust's sometime assistant, Wagner, has created in a test tube, sets out for a night of revelry. In response to Wagner's plaintive question, "And what about me?" he replies: "As for you, you'll have to

44. Wer will was Lebendigs erkennen und beschreiben, / Sucht erst den Geist heraus zu treiben, / Dann hat er die Teile in seiner Hand, / Fehlt leider! nur das geistige Band.

On this passage, Cassirer 1963, 69–70.

45. Ich weiß es wohl, bejahrt und noch Student, / Bemooster Herr! Auch ein gelehrter Mann / Studiert so fort, weil er nicht anders kann. / So baut man sich ein mäßig Kartenhaus, / Der größte Geist baut's doch nicht völlig aus.

46. Wenn, alter Herr, nicht Lethes trübe Fluten / Das schiefgesenkte, kahle Haupt durchschwommen, / Seht anerkennend hier den Schüler kommen, / Entwachsen akademischen Ruten. / Ich find' Euch noch, wie ich Euch sah; / Ein anderer bin i c h wieder da.

stay at home and do the most important work of all. Unroll your old parchments, collect the vital elements according to the prescription, and mix them carefully with one another. Pay attention to the What and, still more, pay attention to the How" (6987–92).[47] But for his part, the Homunculus is out to acquire "wealth, honor, fame, a long and healthy life—and, perhaps, knowledge and virtue" (6997–98), but evidently in that order of priority. Meanwhile, the living caricature of a scholar, the Pedant at the end of Part Two, Act I, on seeing the vision of Helen of Troy in the flesh, can only blurt out, "Above all I must stick to the text," and proliferate his footnote references to Homer's *Iliad*, while being obliged to admit nevertheless: "I am not young, but I do find her pleasing" (6536–40).

Yet even for Faust as natural scientist and pantheist, such a reduction of Nature to a taxonomy of species according to the arbitrary categories of the learned has never been enough. Turning the tables on Mephistopheles, Faust calls him a "pedant" for requiring written documentation of their pact (1716). The outbreak of the forces of Nature in a storm, he tells the Earth Spirit, has always had the effect of revealing "me to myself, and mysterious and profound wonders manifest themselves to my own breast" (3233–34), thus of providing insights into the human heart no less than into the heart of Earth and of Nature. This leads him eventually to the apotheosis of a "feeling," beyond name and beyond description, inspired by his love for Margarete: "When I have feelings, and when I look for a name to describe my feelings and my upheaval, but find none, then I roam around through the whole world with all my senses, groping for the most exalted words, and call this ardor that burns within me infinite, eternal, eternal"; such a sense of reverence, he is confident, cannot be "a trick of devilish stealth" (3059–66).[48] To Margarete he articulates even more fer-

47. Eh nun, / Du bleibst zu Hause, Wichtigstes zu tun. / Entfalte du die alten Pergamente, / Nach Vorschrift sammle Lebenselemente / Und füge sie mit Vorsicht eins ans andre. / Das Was bedenke, mehr bedenke Wie.

48. Wenn ich empfinde, / Für das Gefühl, für das Gewühl / Nach Namen suche, keinen finde, / Dann durch die Welt mit allen Sinnen schweife, / Nach allen höchsten Worten greife, / Und diese Glut, von der ich brenne, / Unendlich, ewig, ewig nenne, / Ist das ein teuflisch Lügenspiel?

vently and more poetically his sense that this is an experience of eternity itself: "To surrender completely and to feel a delight that must be eternal! Eternal—its end would be despair. No, it has no end! No end!" That eternity is so transcendent as to be "inexpressible" (3190–94).[49] For the same reason, his love for Margarete becomes to him, alongside the traditional cosmological arguments, a proof for the existence of God, though with the conclusion: "Feeling is all!" (3446–58).

But all of this in the first instance leads Faust to the recrudescence of the darker side of polytheism and the supernatural, which is the preoccupation with the black arts.[50] As Mephistopheles says in his speech, if "deceit and sorcery" can supplant "reason and science," then the devil can achieve dominion (1851–55). Sometimes, to be sure, the language about enchantment seems to be little more than the hyperbole of young love. Thus when Faust visits Margarete's bedroom, he can exclaim, though she is not even there: "Am I surrounded here by some fragrance of enchantment?" (2721)—a question that appears already in *Urfaust* (573). Similarly, when Margarete recalls her intimacy with Faust, she revels in "the magic flow of his words, the touch of his hands—and his kiss!" (3398–3401). This is in keeping with Faust's use of God-language in speaking about her: she has a "chaste countenance of heaven," and the message of the flower petals, "He loves me— loves me not," ought to serve as a "divine oracle" to her (3182–85). In the polemic against the use of paper money—in which, according to Eckermann, Goethe "derives paper money from Mephistopheles and thus so significantly attaches himself to an important issue of the day and makes it eternal"[51]—currency is described by the Court Jester as "the leaves of the sorcerer" (6157). Even Christian symbols can be used for the purposes of magic. Mephistopheles

49. Sich hinzugeben ganz und eine Wonne / Zu fühlen, die ewig sein muß! / Ewig!—Ihr Ende würde Verzweiflung sein. / Nein, kein Ende! Kein Ende!

50. Aron 1912–13, 33:42–66; 34:34–63, is a helpful summary of Goethe's attitude to superstition, including astrology.

51. Eckermann, *Gespräche mit Goethe*, Part Two, 27 December 1829 (Bergemann 1987, 356); the issue is examined in Binswanger 1985.

is unable to cross the threshold of Faust's study to leave because of
the restraint of "the mandrake's foot in the doorway," which Faust
identifies as a "pentagram," perhaps an inscription of the five
letters of the name "Jesus" used as an amulet (1395–96).[52] But
beyond the conventional invocation of supernatural terms for
purely natural sentiments—which is also evident, for example, in
what such terms of magic as "enchanting" and "charming" have
come to mean in many modern languages—Faust's pilgrimage
brings him face to face with authentic witchcraft and into a captiv-
ity to it.[53]

Thus a sentiment expressed by the Herald early in Part Two
has already been hovering over much of Part One: "Yet I am afraid
that airy ghosts are coming in through the windows, and I would
not have the skill to liberate you from spooks and sorcery" (5500–
5503).[54] The attitude of Faust the rational scientist to these black
arts is quite ambivalent. Thus he recalls—with an almost alchemi-
cal mixture of whimsy, fondness, irony, and bitterness—that his
own father was an alchemist-physician, well-meaning and even
expert in a manner of speaking, but ultimately ineffectual: "Living
in obscurity but with integrity, my father reflected about Nature
and her sacred spheres in a capricious and idiosyncratic but honest
fashion. He joined a society of alchemists who went in for the black
kitchen, following infinite recipes to mix opposites in search of
remedies" (1034–41).[55] Of course, he adds, this superstitious and
yet scientific research of his father's sometimes had an outcome
different from the intended one, because "this was the remedy, the
patients died" (1048). At times, therefore, these magical powers are
something offensive and even loathsome to him. Mephistopheles is
able to effect various cures by his black magic (6319–66). That

52. An informative explanation in Bennett 1986, 73–78.

53. Lepinte 1957 is a discussion of Goethe's attitude to "occultism."

54. Doch ich fürchte, durch die Fenster / Ziehen luftige Gespenst-
er, / Und von Spuk und Zaubereien / Wüßt' ich euch nicht zu befreien.

55. Mein Vater war ein dunkler Ehrenmann, / Der über die Natur und ihre
heil'gen Kreise / In Redlichkeit, jedoch auf seine Weise, / Mit grillenhafter
Mühe sann; / Der, in Gesellschaft von Adepten, / Sich in die schwarze Küche
schloß / Und, nach unendlichen Rezepten, / Das Widrige zusammengoß.

same black magic causes several kinds of wine to flow spontaneously from a table in Auerbach's Cellar in Leipzig (2245–2336).[56] It may be a significant index of the maturation of the work that in *Urfaust* Faust himself performs this trick, whereas in the final version Mephistopheles does; for in the final version Faust exclaims, upon entering the Witch's Kitchen, "I am repelled by this insane sorcery!"[57] He asks whether their contract requires him from now on, under the mentorship of Mephistopheles, to be forced to rely on such stunts, putting the question: "Do you mean to say that Nature or some noble spirit has not discovered a cure?" (2337–46).[58] At this stage at any rate, his own existential commitment continues to be to Nature, not to witchcraft; for it is often the case that, as he explains much later to the Emperor in Part Two, Act IV, "Nature functions in such a sovereign and free way that the clergy in their stupidity call it sorcery" (10453–54), a remark that manages to take a swipe at sorcery and at the orthodox Christian clergy at the same time. Yet when the Lord Treasurer says, "I choose the sorcerer as my colleague," that seems to refer to Faust; for the stage directions add: "Exit, with Faust" (6142), who is now apparently to be identified as a sorcerer.

Nevertheless, in the course of their peregrinations Faust issues the challenge to Mephistopheles: "To get us in here, do you intend this time to represent yourself as a sorcerer or as a devil?" (4060–61), which suggests some continuing distinction between "sorcerer" and "devil." Yet in speaking this way, Faust does not refer explicitly to his earlier flirtations with such sorcery. He had taken up magic, he has explained near the beginning of the drama, "to get an insight into what holds the world together at its inner depths" (377–83),[59] that is, in the service of the very quest for the

---

56. Brief comments, especially on the medieval background, by Salomon 1960, 531–40.

57. Mir widersteht das tolle Zauberwesen!

58. Hat die Natur und hat ein edler Geist / Nicht irgendeinen Balsam ausgefunden?

Bartscherer 1911, 169–70, provides some explanation especially of the "Balsam."

59. Daß ich erkenne, was die Welt / Im Innersten zusammenhält.

meaning of the world "at its inner depths" that has inspired his scientific and pansophic studies. Or, as he specifies a few lines earlier, "This is why I have given myself over to magic, to see if, through the power and the speaking of the Spirit, I can get an insight into many a mystery" (377–79).[60] In this sense the natural scientist as pantheist and the poetic artist as polytheist seem to share the same goal of probing "many a mystery," differing, at least to some degree, in the means employed to attain that goal. When Faust expresses the wish for a "sorcerer's cloak" (1122), Wagner warns him about the dangers lurking in this means: "Do not summon up that all-too familiar host, which swarms and spreads through the air and threatens people with thousandfold danger from every side. They are glad to listen to us, because they are full of mischief. They are glad to obey us, because they like to deceive us. They pretend to come from heaven and they whisper in *englisch* as they lie to us" (1126–41)[61]—the word *englisch* referring here not to the English language (which demons presumably can also speak) but to the capacity of Satan, as the New Testament says, to "masquerade as an angel of light."[62]

For that matter, whatever the linkage in Faust's phrase about Mephistopheles, "sorcerer or devil" (4060–61), may connote, the attitude toward magic and superstition articulated by Mephistopheles is, ironically, not without a certain ambivalence, which is in keeping with his character as, in Faust's words, "a spirit of contradiction" (4030), or as, in his own words earlier, "the spirit who always negates" (1338). Thus when he says of Margarete's friend Marthe, "That is a woman destined for pandering and gypsy ways!" (3029–30), the condescension and contempt are evident; for

60. Drum hab' ich mich der Magie ergeben, / Ob mir durch Geistes Kraft und Mund / Nicht manch Geheimnis würde kund.

Birven 1924, and Wilhelm Resenhöfft in Mahal 1973, 69–98, are devoted to the theme of magic.

61. Berufe nicht die wohlbekannte Schar, / Die strömend sich im Dunstkreis überbreitet, / Dem Menschen tausendfältige Gefahr, / Von allen Enden her, bereitet. . . . / Sie hören gern, zum Schaden froh gewandt, / Gehorchen gern, weil sie uns gern betrügen; / Sie stellen wie vom Himmel sich gesandt, / Und lispeln englisch, wenn sie lügen.

62. 2 Cor. 11:14.

it is already clear that toying with witchcraft and divination is a superstition characteristic of the uneducated classes (872–83). But so is the guilt by association of the pious and superstitious soul who "complains of 'sorcery' if all at once the sole of his foot begins to itch or if he stumbles" (4982–84).[63] And Mephistopheles, when Faust requires of him that he summon Helen of Troy from the world beyond, seems to identify a class structure within that world, between the proletarian spooks cultivated among the common people of the North and an elitist Classical "goddess [Göttin]" of the South like Helen. "With witches' switches, ghastly ghosts, or dwarf deformities, I could be of service immediately," he explains. "But the devil's darlings, though nothing to be despised, are not on a par with Classical heroines. . . . These pagans of antiquity are no business of mine. They inhabit a hell of their own" (6199–6210).[64] The cryptic explanation of Mephistopheles to Faust, that there is a natural means to rejuvenate him but that this "belongs to another book and to a strange chapter in it" (2348–50), could also be taken as a disparagement, on the devil's part, of the "madness of sorcery" that Faust has just denounced (2337), together with a grudging admiration for the natural means as somehow preferable. Much later, watching the members of the court gather from all corners of the ancient spirit world in the Brightly Lit Halls, Mephistopheles sounds a similar note of disparagement, "Here, I would suppose, there is no need of magic formulas" (6375), perhaps because they would be ineffective.

While he is pursuing his quest for knowledge even on the Nordic Walpurgis Night, Faust sees the possibility that Satan worship might be the key to deeper insight, as he glimpses a group of its devotees: "Yet I would rather be up there on top. Already I can see the glow and the whirling smoke. There is the crowd, streaming up to the Evil One. That must be the place to solve many a

63. That sentiment is repeated in the superstitious suspicions of Baucis (11113–14), which in her case, however, prove to be accurate.

64. Mit Hexen-Fexen, mit Gespenst-Gespinsten, / Kielkröpfigen Zwergen steh' ich gleich zu Diensten; / Doch Teufels-Liebchen, wenn auch nicht zu schelten, / Sie können nicht für Heroinen gelten. . . . / Das Heidenvolk geht mich nichts an, / Es haust in seiner eignen Hölle.

riddle." But Mephistopheles warns him off such a quest with the caution: "But also to hook up with many a riddle" (4037–41). Soon thereafter the true character of Satan worship becomes clear in the song of the Epigrams (who take their name, "Xenien," from Goethe's collection of epigrams): "We are here as insects with sharp little claws, to honor Satan, our Papa, as he deserves" (4303–6). When, earlier in the action, the Will-o'-the-wisp warns Mephistopheles that "the mountain today is mad with witchcraft, and if a will-o'-the-wisp is to show you the way, you mustn't ask for too much precision" (3868–70), the communication between these two nonhumans conveys an almost human sense of foreboding about the presence and power of the supernatural. Yet Mephistopheles and the Will-o'-the-Wisp can also sing antiphonally with Faust (although Goethe does not indicate who sings which verse),[65] Faust apparently being the singer of the opening words: "We have, it seems, entered the sphere of dreams and of sorcery" (3871–72). That "sphere of sorcery" is in many ways a reverse image of the real and divine world. As poetic artist and polytheist, Faust might have invoked the Muses, as the Poet in the Prelude on the Stage almost does after his own fashion (63–66); but in this universe of reversed images the Leader of the Muses can exclaim: "I would be only too happy to lose myself in this crowd of witches, because I would rather lead them than the Muses" (4311–14).

Nor is it only to the Classical Muses that the witches stand in such a relation, but there is also an ironic counterpoint between them and the heavenly angels. In the sublime hymn of the Prologue in Heaven, the Choir of Angels sings to God the Creator, in words quoted earlier: "The very sight of it gives strength to the angels, because thou art unfathomable, and all thy sublime works are as glorious as they were on the first day" (267–70).[66] But, as already here in the Prologue in Heaven Mephistopheles parodies this angelic song (281–82) and as in a later scene in Part Two the Sphinxes parody the song of the Sirens (7156–65), so in the Wal-

65. C. Thomas 1892–97, 1:326, is a concise summary of the problem.
66. Der Anblick gibt den Engeln Stärke, / Da keiner dich ergründen mag, / Und alle deine hohen Werke / Sind herrlich wie am ersten Tag.

purgis Night scene the Choir of Witches intones what seems to be a parody of those angelic words, and in a similar meter: "The salve gives courage to the witches. A rag will do for a sail, any trough will do for a boat. Anyone who does not fly in the air today, never will" (4008–11).[67] If the figure of Plutus in the Carnival scene is in fact Faust in allegorical disguise,[68] there is special significance to the words that follow his invocation of the forces of Nature: "If spirits threaten to do us harm, magic will have to get busy" (5985–86). For here the powers of magic and sorcery, which belong to the world of Mephistopheles as "sorcerer or devil" (4060–61), are put to the positive use óf "a purely poetic magic,"[69] as they were already put to use as an instrumentality in the cause of science by Faust's early effort to invoke magic (377–79).

The stage directions for the Carnival in Act I of Part Two specify, after having introduced "various poets, poets of nature, courtly and knightly bards, lyricists as well as rhapsodists" (at 5295): "The poets of the night and the graveyard ask to be excused, because they are engaged in a most interesting conversation with a newly arrived vampire, the outcome of which might be the development of a new form of poetry; the Herald is obliged to go along with it, and meanwhile he invokes Greek mythology, which even in modern garb remains true to character and retains its appeal" (at 5299).[70]

Commentators have, quite rightly it would seem, connected this passage with Goethe's statement in Eckermann's *Conversations with Goethe,* which was itself part of a lengthy disquisition about French literature there but which also well characterized Goethe's opinion of German "graveyard Romantics": "People are beginning to regard as boring the portrayal of noble feelings and

67. Die Salbe gibt den Hexen Mut, / Ein Lumpen ist zum Segel gut, / Ein gutes Schiff ist jeder Trog; / Der flieget nie, der heut nicht flog.

68. Schlaffer 1981, 65–78; D. Lohmeyer 1975, 90–93.

69. Emrich 1957, 216–17.

70. Die Nacht- und Grabdichter lassen sich entschuldigen, weil sie soeben im interessantesten Gespräch mit einem frisch entstandenen Vampyren begriffen seien, woraus eine neue Dichtart sich vielleicht entwickeln könnte; der Herold muß es gelten lassen und ruft indessen die griechische Mythologie hervor, die, selbst in moderner Maske, weder Charakter noch Gefälliges verliert.

deeds, and they are making attempts at treating all sorts of atroci-
ties." The end result of this lust for the bizarre and atrocious,
Goethe continued, was that "in place of the beautiful content of
Greek mythology there come devils, witches, and vampires, and
the sublime heroes of antiquity must make room for rogues and
galley slaves."[71] This very antithesis seems to mark the fundamental difference between Faust's participating in the Nordic Walpurgis Night, with its "devils, witches, and vampires," and his
becoming acquainted with the noble gods of Greece on Classical
Walpurgis Night. It should be kept in mind, moreover, that although Goethe did visit Italy in 1786–88 and again in 1790, leaving his *Italian Journey* as a permanent monument, his only ac-
quaintance with Greece was through the literature, art, and history
of the Classical period, for which his *Winckelmann* and above all
this Classical Walpurgis Night are the monuments. As his biogra-
pher has well said, moreover, "Goethe did not spend the years from
1786 to 1788 in Italy, as he much later admitted . . . ; he spent them
in Arcadia, in a creation of his mind and heart, his needs and
longings, into which as much of the real Italy was mixed as was
necessary to convince him that the object of his desires had a place
and habitation on this earth."[72] The same applied in even greater
measure to his idealized version of the Greece he had never even
seen. The antithesis between Greece and the North also underlies
the attribution, to an otherwise unidentified Orthodox Theologian,
of the following anathema: "No claws, no tail! Yet it remains
beyond doubt: He is a devil, just as the gods of Greece are" (4271–
74). This seems to be Goethe's way of caricaturing Friedrich
Leopold, Graf zu Stolberg, who had attacked Schiller's poem "The
Gods of Greece" for its false doctrine and who was himself con-
verted to Roman Catholicism in 1800.[73] Such orthodox hostility to
Classical antiquity echoes the widespread patristic identification of
pagan gods as demons.[74] But in the context of Faust's development

71. Eckermann, *Gespräche mit Goethe*, Part Three, 14 March 1830 (Bergemann 1987, 675).
72. Boyle 1991, 1:653.
73. On Stolberg, see Trunz and Loos 1971, 213–16.
74. Augustine *City of God* XI.1.

it reflects a grave misunderstanding; for, by yet another curious irony, it puts orthodox Christian theology on the same side with Mephistopheles.

The invocation, specifically in the name of poetry, of "Greek mythology" as that which "even in modern garb, remains true to character and retains its appeal" (at 5299) acts as a prelude to the Carnival. It is followed by scenes in which several of the various specific deities of Classical polytheism, inhabitants of "the region of Olympus" (6027), make an appearance. There is the Roman corn goddess Ceres, with her various "gifts to adorn you" (5128). One of the most striking is the goddess Nike, the winged Victory, whom Prudence describes as "up there on the pinnacle, that goddess with her spacious wingspread, ready to move with blessing in all directions. The glitter and glory surrounding her shine into the distance on every side. She is called Victoria, the goddess of all activity" (5449–56).[75] Also among those present are the aquatic Nymphs, "Nereids, curious about this elegant dwelling place" (6022–23), as well as many other deities.

It is in the realm of Zeus (7137), Classical Walpurgis Night— which is Goethe's own artistic creation in Part Two as a counterweight to the traditional Nordic Walpurgis Night of Part One[76]— that the experience of Faust as poetic artist and polytheist attains its zenith. Although Faust plays a significant participatory role only in the scene at the Lower Peneios (7249–7494), the other scenes are, according to Goethe's sketch of December 1826, Faust's "dreams, which take place in detail visibly in the eyes of the beholder."[77] So it is that "the activity of the soul of Faust while asleep directs itself to something impossible that is, in accordance with the rules of poetic composition, treated as possible: to revivify a past occurrence of supreme importance."[78] As the Greek witch

75. Droben aber auf der Zinne / Jene Göttin, mit behenden / Breiten Flügeln, zum Gewinne / Allerseits sich hinzuwenden. / Rings umgibt sie Glanz und Glorie, / Leuchtend fern nach allen Seiten; / Und sie nennet sich Viktorie, / Göttin aller Tätigkeiten.
76. Fairley 1953, 66–86.
77. In Trunz 1968, 439.
78. Kommerell 1944, 41.

Erichtho solemnly intones at the beginning of the Classical Walpurgis Night, "Lured by the rare and wondrous radiance of the
night, the legion of Hellenic legend has gathered" (7027–28). Or,
as the Homunculus exclaims, less solemnly, "As I have suddenly
recalled, this is Classical Walpurgis Night; the best thing that could
possibly happen will bring him into his element!" (6940–43). The
dominant mood of the Classical Walpurgis Night is a poetic aestheticism, for which Helen will be the ultimate embodiment.[79]
Faust's first words on touching Classical soil and finding himself
"by a miracle, here in Greece" (7074) are "Where is she?" (7056,
7070); and again on the Upper Peneios he asks, "Has any one of you
seen Helen?" (7196).[80]

This aestheticism had found its initial embodiment in the
vision of Leda by the Homunculus, even before Classical Walpurgis Night:

> Meaningful! A beautiful surrounding! Limpid waters in a dense
> grove! Women undressing, the most delightful women of all! It gets
> better all the time. But one of them stands out brightly, a woman
> sprung from a line of heroes, or even of gods. She dips her foot in the
> transparent flood, her lovely body's flame cools itself in the yielding,
> glittering wave. But what is that whir of swiftly flapping wings,
> what is that plunging and splashing that shatters the smooth mirror?
> The maidens run away in fright; but only she, the queen, calmly
> looks on and, with a woman's pride and pleasure, watches the prince
> of swans nestle at her knees and, gently insistent, stay. He seems to
> like it there (6903–17).[81]

79. Riemann 1962, 109–34; Busch 1949, 194–200.
80. On Faust in Greece, Hagen 1940, 24–44.
81. Bedeutend! Schön umgeben!—Klar Gewässer / Im dichten Haine!
Fraun, die sich entkleiden, / Die allerliebsten!—Das wird immer besser. / Doch
eine läßt sich glänzend unterscheiden, / Aus höchstem Helden-, wohl aus Göt-
terstamme. / Sie setzt den Fuß in das durchsichtige Helle; / Des edlen Körpers
holde Lebensflamme / Kühlt sich im schmiegsamen Kristall der Welle.—
/ Doch welch Getöse rasch bewegter Flügel, / Welch Sausen, Plätschern wühlt
im glatten Spiegel? / Die Mädchen fliehn verschüchtert; doch allein / Die Königin, sie blickt gelassen drein / Und sieht mit stolzem weiblichem Vergnügen /
Der Schwäne Fürsten ihrem Knie sich schmiegen, / Zudringlich-zahm. Er
scheint sich zu gewöhnen.
The place of this vision in the drama is treated by Parkes-Perret 1984, 244–49;
on the background of this account, which seems to be based on Correggio's
painting of this incident in Classical mythology, Samson Eitrem in Pauly-Wissowa
1893–1963, 12:1116–25.

Leda is only the first stage of the process. For then, during the Classical Walpurgis Night itself, this poetic aestheticism attaches itself to Galatea, who is being worshiped as a goddess: "Now, borne along on the iridescence of Venus's scallop-shell chariot, comes Galatea, the fairest of them all, who, ever since Cypris [Venus] turned away from us, has been worshiped in Paphos as a goddess and who, as the heir, possesses her temple-city and chariot-throne" (8144–49).[82] This designation of her as "the fairest of them all" and as "a goddess" here in the Classical Walpurgis Night of Part Two, Act II, has been anticipated in Part Two, Act I, when, after Faust has called up the apparitions from the past, the Astrologer exclaims, on seeing Paris: "I do believe the whole temple is singing. The mist is dropping, and out of the thin veil a beautiful young man steps forward with measured step. Here my task is finished, for I don't need to name him. Who could fail to recognize the noble Paris!" (6448–52).[83] Leda and Galatea are ultimately stand-ins for Helen. Soon thereafter, therefore, the Astrologer recognizes the apparition of Helen of Troy, and once more he exclaims: "The beautiful one is coming: if I only had tongues of fire! Much has been sung for a long time in praise of beauty. Anyone to whom she appears is caught up in rapture, and anyone who would possess her would receive an excess of happiness" (6483–86).[84]

Yet the Classical Walpurgis Night fairly swarms with supernatural beings of every variety, no less than did the Nordic Walpurgis Night: "The mountain is already teeming with myrmidons, dwelling in the fissures of the rocks—pygmies, ants, Tom Thumbs, and other little busybodies" (7873–76). In fact, Faust

82. Im Farbenspiel von Venus' Muschelwagen / Kommt Galatee, die Schönste, nun getragen, / Die, seit sich Kypris von uns abgekehrt, / In Paphos wird als Göttin selbst verehrt. / Und so besitzt die Holde lange schon, / Als Erbin, Tempelstadt und Wagenthron.
Emrich 1957, 301, and especially Neumann 1985, 223–53, locate Galatea in the plot of the drama.

83. Ich glaube gar, der ganze Tempel singt. / Das Dunstige senkt sich; aus dem leichten Flor / Ein schöner Jüngling tritt im Takt hervor. / Hier schweigt mein Amt, ich brauch' ihn nicht zu nennen, / Wer sollte nicht den holden Paris kennen!

84. Die Schöne kommt, und hätt' ich Feuerzungen!— / Von Schönheit ward von jeher viel gesungen— / Wem sie erscheint, wird aus sich selbst entrückt, / Wem sie gehörte, ward zu hoch beglückt.

himself and his companion, the centaur Chiron, are here identified by Manto as "demigods" (7473). The Nymphs appear again here (7263–70, 8044–57), followed by those who dwell "in the hollow foot of Olympus" (7491) and those who "are to be inquired after on Olympus" (8197). Thus, *pace* Goethe's theory that an alienation from Classical antiquity means that "in place of the beautiful content of Greek mythology there come devils, witches, and vampires," there are not only some witches in the Classical Walpurgis Night but vampires as well, as Mephistopheles notes with some glee upon contacting the Phorcyads, sea demons spoken of in Hesiod and in Aeschylus (who even wrote a play, now lost, about them).[85] Mephistopheles senses a greater affinity with the Phorcyads than with most of the other supernatural beings of Greek "paganism" (6209): "Here it is, rooted in the land of beauty, the land celebrated with the name 'antiquity.' They are stirring, they seem to sense me, they are twittering in whistles, like vampire bats" (7978–81). In fact, he even takes on the appearance of a "Phorcyad in profile" for a while (8012–33).[86]

This reaction of Mephistopheles is part of yet another of the "very seriously intended jests": the culture shock of Mephistopheles in the guise of a tourist in Classical Greece. The Homunculus warns him that "the Northwest, Satan, is your playground, but this time we are sailing southeast" (6950–51). But initially, at the outset of the Classical Walpurgis Night, he professes to find continuity between his demonic world and Classical paganism, declaring: "If here I see altogether appalling ghosts, as I do when I look through old windows in the waste and gloom of the North, I shall feel as much at home here as I do there" (7044–47). Once more, he asserts the continuity as he locates himself between the Sphinxes, finding it "easy and comfortable to get settled here, because I can understand every one of you" (7112–13). But after further questions and riddles, the Sphinx says to him: "You may stay forever if you wish, but you'll soon want to leave our company of your own accord. In your own country you do as you please, but if I'm not mistaken, you are uncomfortable here" (7142–45). Yet

85. Hans Johannes in Pauly-Wissowa 1893–1963, S 9:827–28.
86. Schüpbach 1980, 269–85.

again, he tries to accommodate himself to the supernatural world of Greece, and, on being greeted by Empusa, seems to have found a long-lost relative: "I thought there would be nothing here, but, alas! I am finding close relatives. It is an old story: From Harz to Hellas, cousins all the way!" (7740–43).[87] Nevertheless, he is compelled to acknowledge that Classical antiquity is too "vivid" for him (7087) and that he still prefers the company of Northern witches to that of these sisters from Thessaly. "I always knew how to get the upper hand with Northern witches," he explains, "but I can't get used to these foreign spirits. The Blocksberg remains a completely comfortable locale, where you can fit in wherever you happen to be" (7676–79). As for the sisters from Thessaly, he is willing to deal with them only temporarily. He has been been "inquiring about them for a long time," these "witches of Thessaly." And although he "would not find it comfortable to live with them night after night, a visit is worth a try" (6979–83). For with some reluctance he must confess that "if there were no witches, who the devil would want to be a devil?" (7724–25). In a curious way, although admitting that "of course we, too, are indecent to the core," Mephistopheles owns up to finding "Classical antiquity too vivid" and manifests a prudish abhorrence at the Classical Greek lack of inhibition about nudity and sex: "I find myself completely alienated. Almost everyone naked, and only one here and there with a shirt on: the Sphinxes indecent, the Griffins shameless, and then the whole crowd, hairy and winged, catching your eye in front or from behind" (7081–87).[88] He had long since expressed his disgust with the human body in any form; as he says early on, speaking about the power of light: "It streams from bodies, it makes bodies beautiful, it is intercepted by a body. And so, I hope, it will not last long and will perish when bodies do" (1355–58).[89]

87. Hier dacht' ich lauter Unbekannte / Und finde leider Nahverwandte; / Es ist ein altes Buch zu blättern: / Vom Harz bis Hellas immer Vettern!

88. So find' ich mich doch ganz und gar entfremdet, / Fast alles nackt, nur hie und da behemdet: / Die Sphinxe schamlos, unverschämt die Greife, / Und was nicht alles, lockig und beflügelt, / Von vorn und hinten sich im Auge spiegelt.

89. Von Körpern strömt's, die Körper macht es schön, / Ein Körper hemmt's auf seinem Gange, / So, hoff' ich, dauert es nicht lange, / Und mit den Körpern wird's zugrunde gehn.

Even the benign climate of Greece and its unfamiliar smells repel him, by contrast with his home territory in the Harz Mountains, where the air is "resinous [harzig]": "Here I have to drag myself up a steep and rocky climb and stumble over the stiff roots of these old oaks. In my Harz Mountains there's a resinous atmosphere with a touch of pitch in it, which is what I enjoy, next after sulphur. . . . Here, among these Greeks, there is almost no trace of anything like that" (7951–56). For, as he said in Faust's (former) laboratory even before the opening of Classical Walpurgis Night and as he has better reason to believe now that he has had the direct experience, "That Greek nation has never been worth very much!" (6972). Or, as he says in reflection on the entire situation, "It does seem that I have not grown any wiser. Absurdity here, absurdity in the North. Ghosts are as perverted here as they are there, and poets and people just as crude" (7791–94), which, presumably, is meant to include Faust (and Goethe) as poet. "Thus with strange inevitability," as one critic has noted the ironic twist, "Goethe's longing for a higher and purer style in life and art, that led him to despise the northern world around him, was driven to take refuge with that most northern, least Grecian symbol of himself: with Faust."[90]

Glamorized though it is, this polytheism shows its more sinister aspects in each of these three episodes—Walpurgis Night with Walpurgis Night's Dream, Carnival, and Classical Walpurgis Night—as the early reference to the idolatry of the golden calf already suggests (5041). One of the most persistent elements of continuity between the three episodes is the decisive role of magic and sorcery. Already in the Dark Gallery, Mephistopheles makes the continuation of that element explicit when he says to Faust (apparently alluding also to the quest for Helen of Troy, which Faust will accomplish by his own powers): "You can summon hero and heroine from out of the night, as the first to accomplish that deed. When it is done, you will be the one who has achieved it. Then immediately, in accordance with magical procedure, the cloud of incense must be transformed into gods" (6298–6302). In the Baronial Hall between the Carnival and the Classical Wal-

90. Trevelyan 1981, 239–40.

purgis Night, the Astrologer sets the stage for such sorcery and magic: "Let the drama begin its course. The master commands it, open up, you walls! With magic available, there is nothing more standing in the way. The carpets are disappearing as if they were curled up in fire. The wall splits and turns around. A deep stage seems to appear, and a mysterious light seems to be illumining us. And I am mounting the proscenium" (6391–98). Mephistopheles finds all of this quite encouraging. "From here on," he says, "I hope for universal approval, because prompting is the devil's rhetoric" (6399–6400), even if it has to be in Greece.

These aspects of polytheism are all the more menacing because, especially "in the land of beauty," Classical Greece, they give the appearance of being something beautiful. For example, "You will not recognize those who are now arriving, regardless of how learned you are in ancient writings. To look at them, despite all the evil they commit, you would call them welcome guests." These are the Furies in the Carnival, who are "pretty, with good figures, friendly" (5345–50). Once again, it is the Astrologer who sounds the theme, as he carries out the solemn induction of Faust "in priestly garb" as "a miracle man" and intones: "Receive with reverence the hours that have been granted by the stars. Let rationality be restricted by magic words; and, instead, let fantasy, rich and free, come from far away and rule us. Gaze now at what you had boldly demanded. It is impossible; therefore it is credible" (6415–20).[91] Once again, at one stroke this affirms, with the words "Let rationality be restricted by magic words," the portentous attack of Mephistopheles on "reason and science" (1851–55), and does so by invoking, with the words "It is impossible; therefore it is credible," the anti-intellectualist formula of traditional Christian orthodoxy, both Catholic and Protestant: "credo quia impossibile."[92] For these are spirits that defy and surpass any human "reason and science," and even the traditional human fine arts, as

91. Empfangt mit Ehrfurcht sterngegönnte Stunden; / Durch magisch Wort sei die Vernunft gebunden; / Dagegen weit heran bewege frei / Sich herrliche verwegne Phantasei. / Mit Augen schaut nun, was ihr kühn begehrt, / Unmöglich ist's, drum eben glaubenswert.

92. Originally from Tertullian On the Flesh of Christ 5: "Certum est quia impossibile est."

the Herald acknowledges: "The secret activity of the spirits hinders me from my old occupation of announcing the play. It is useless to try to account for the confusion that prevails on any understandable grounds" (6377–80). Later on, in Act III of Part Two, the Choir celebrates the return of Helen to the Palace of Menelaus with a hymn to the gods of Classical polytheism: "Praise the holy gods for restoring good fortune and granting such homecomings!" (8619–21).[93] But this leads the Choir eventually to a special version of the Hellenic tradition, in which Greek rationality and the search for truth—"reason and science"—have been subordinated to a poetic polytheism: "Everything that happens in our own days is a poor imitation of the glorious ancestral days. Your story cannot be compared with the one that an amiable lie, more believable than truth, sang about the son of Maia" (9637–44).[94] The reference to "an amiable lie, more believable than truth," is reminiscent of the "likely story" in Plato's *Timaeus* as a description of the myth of creation.[95] But there is perhaps no "amiable lie" more ubiquitous in the tradition of Classical poetic polytheism than the doctrine of the influence of the stars on human destiny.[96] It is possible for the Emperor to refer to this doctrine quite without self-consciousness, "You are assembling under the sign of a favorable star. Good fortune and success have been decreed for us from above" (4763–64), and for Faust, addressing the Emperor, to mention it casually (10450).[97] But the stars, too, are closely bound up with Classical mythology. In response to the question of a Sphinx, "Do you have

93. Preiset die heiligen, / Glücklich herstellenden / Und heimführenden Götter!

94. Alles, was je geschieht / Heutigen Tages, / Trauriger Nachklang ist's / Herrlicher Ahnherrntage; / Nicht vergleicht sich dein Erzählen / Dem, was liebliche Lüge, / Glaubhaftiger als Wahrheit, / Von dem Sohne sang der Maja.

"The son of Maia" was Hermes.

95. Cornford 1957, 28–32.

96. Bartscherer 1911, 183–213, and Schiff 1927, 86–96, are among the few studies dealing with this topic in Goethe's *Faust;* although the essay "Die sittliche Astrologie der Makarie in 'Wilhelm Meisters Wanderjahren,'" Spranger 1946, 192–206, is addressed directly to *Wilhelm Meister,* it pertains also to the ambiguous place of astrology in *Faust.* K. Thomas 1971, 283–385, deals specifically with England, but it sheds light on the period immediately preceding Goethe's time in other countries as well.

97. Wattenberg 1969, 102–9, considers this question.

any lore about the stars? What do you say about the present hour?"
Mephistopheles is obliged to content himself with some evasive
observations about shooting stars and a clipped moon (7125–27).
For an explanation of their power, therefore, he appeals to the
authority of the learned Astrologer (4947–50). The Astrologer in
turn recites the names of the heavenly bodies, which are, not
coincidentally, the names of the deities of polytheism and which
carry out the functions of those deities: "As for the sun itself, it is
sheer gold. Mercury the messenger performs his service for pleasure and profit. Lady Venus is putting it over all of you, as, both
early and late, she gazes at you lovingly. Luna is chaste and moody.
Even if Mars does not hit you, his power is a threat to you. Jupiter
remains the most beautiful in his glow. Saturn is large, but to the
eye he seems distant and small" (4955–62).[98]

Later, Mephistopheles pays tribute to the Astrologer's science,
by which he can "know the sequence in which the stars move"
(6401). The Astrologer refers to "the hours that have been granted
by the stars," which are to be received "with reverence" (6415).
Faust's mocking words "Yes, all the way to the stars!" (574) in
response to Wagner's praise of the study of history, "It is very
gratifying to transport oneself into the spirit of the times, to look at
what some wise man before our time once thought, and then to see
what wonderful progress we have finally made" (570–73),[99] had
contained no hint of this more awesome significance of "the stars,"
although it was anticipated already in Faust's opening monologue:
"Then you will be acquainted with the course of the stars; and if
Nature instructs you, you will acquire the power of soul to discern
how one spirit speaks to another" (422–25).[100] But that optimistic

98. Die Sonne selbst, sie ist ein lautres Gold, / Merkur, der Bote, dient um
Gunst und Sold, / Frau Venus hat's euch allen angetan, / So früh als spat blickt
sie euch lieblich an; / Die keusche Luna launet grillenhaft; / Mars, trifft er nicht,
so dräut euch seine Kraft. / Und Jupiter bleibt doch der schönste Schein, / Saturn
ist groß, dem Auge fern und klein.

99. . . . Es ist ein groß Ergetzen, / Sich in den Geist der Zeiten zu
versetzen; / Zu schauen, wie vor uns ein weiser Mann gedacht, / Und wie wir's
dann zuletzt so herrlich weit gebracht.

100. Erkennest dann der Sterne Lauf, / Und wenn Natur dich unter-
weist, / Dann geht die Seelenkraft dir auf, / Wie spricht ein Geist zum andern
Geist.

sense of continuity with the stars and with the All seems to give way in Part Two to a far more ambiguous sense of the influence of fate and chance over the course of human life, indeed over the gods themselves. When Faust was watching the sea, as "it swelled up in order to raise itself up as a tower, and then relented, spilling its waves to ravage the breadth of the flat beach with a storm" (10199–10201), he has to admit that he "regarded it as an accident" (10206). But the "accident" or *tychē* takes on a much more ominous tone as part of the polytheistic pantheon when one of the Phorcyads—or, because he has taken over the "figure" of one of them "for a short time" (8017–18), Mephistopheles speaking through one of the Phorcyads—says to Helen: "To anyone who recollects long years of varied fortune, the highest favor of the gods will seem a dream" (8843–44). Or, to invoke the typology in this book, the stars, which are the proper sphere for the research of the natural scientist, have power over the gods, which are the proper sphere of the poetic artist.

It is, nevertheless, the power of the poet that manages to prevail. For although it seems to be tied, with inseparable bonds, to the cult of the many gods, it survives even when they do not. The same Phorcyad, anticipating a *Götterdämmerung* in which the truth of aestheticism will triumph over what the Choir calls "an amiable lie, more believable than truth" (9642–43), proclaims, to the accompaniment of musical strings, the dawning of a new day in which the poet's celebration of the "heart" will outlive the poet's celebration of the "gods" of polytheism: "Listen to the loveliest of sounds. Set yourselves free from fables. Let go of the crowd of your old gods, their time is past. No one will understand you any more, we demand a higher reward. Whatever is to move the heart must come from the heart" (9679–86).[101] In a curious way, this is a confirmation of Faust's own early sense that the God of the heart could exercise a claim even when a supposedly transcendent Deity

101. Höret allerliebste Klänge, / Macht euch schnell von Fabeln frei! / Eurer Götter alt Gemenge, / Laßt es hin, es ist vorbei. / Niemand will euch mehr verstehen, / Fordern wir doch höhern Zoll: / Denn es muß von Herzen gehen, / Was auf Herzen wirken soll.

could not (1566–69), and of his still earlier warning to Wagner, "You will never connect heart to heart if it does not come from your own heart" (544–45). It is also a confirmation of his repeated recognition that authentic beauty far transcends the powers of sorcery and magic. That beauty is represented ultimately by the Eternal Feminine, but it is represented here by Helen as its Greek expression, complete with her Classical meters.[102] As he says when the real Helen appears, as distinct from the Helen whom he saw with the aid of the devil's sorcery, "The lovely form that once made me feel ecstatic and fortunate when it appeared in the sorcerer's mirror was only a shadowy figure of such beauty!" (6495–97).[103] And therefore, in an evident echo of the formula in his pact with Mephistopheles—"If ever I say to any moment, 'Bide a while! You are so beautiful!'" (1699–1700)—it is to Helen that he declares: "Being itself, even if it is only for one moment, represents a duty" (9418), although it is not until his dying breath that he pronounces the precise formula of the pact (11581–86). For in these two issues—freedom from fate and chance, and freedom from sorcery —the poetic artist as polytheist, with his divine "flame of an overwhelming spiritual power" (9624), needs the illumination that comes from the moral philosopher as monotheist if the abiding values of poetic and aesthetic polytheism (as well as those of scientific pantheism) are to be preserved and made sublime.

102. Trevelyan 1981, 239–62; on the meters of the several scenes involving Helen, the observations of Hamlin 1976, 214 n. 2; 215 n. 8; 225 n. 6; 232 n. 5.

103. Die Wohlgestalt, die mich voreinst entzückte, / In Zauberspiegelung beglückte, / War nur ein Schaumbild solcher Schöne!

CHAPTER FOUR

The Moral Philosopher as Monotheist

FOR GOETHE'S *Faust* as a drama, if not always for Faust as a character in that drama, science and poetry are and remain necessary to the definition of what makes human beings human; to reject one or the other is either to despise "reason and science" as the highest power of which humanity is capable (1851–52) or to blaspheme "Sacred Poesy" (9863). Nevertheless, Faust's spiritual development shows that science and poetry, although necessary, are not sufficient, separately or even together. So, too, both the pantheism of the science and the polytheism of the poetry do not lose their validity for him in the course of his development, and in this sense it would be wrong to treat them as chronological "stages." But they are also insufficient to provide the ultimate justification for the moral "striving" in which that development finds its fulfillment, for this can be provided only by a Goethean version of monotheism. They are—borrowing and extending a metaphor first employed by Mephistopheles in quite another context for the intellectual development of the Baccalaureus (6729–30) and then invoked by the Boy Souls about Faust in the closing scene of the drama (11982)—a "pupa state," through which he passes as does a chrysalis, changing and yet not losing his continuity and identity.[1] The relation both of Faust as natural scientist and of Faust as poetic artist to his eventual position as moral philosopher is, therefore, developmental but dialectical, and the same is true of the relation both of his pantheism and of his polytheism to his eventual monotheism.

The connection between science and morality in Faust's understanding at the opening of the drama is, at best, tenuous; for he says about himself, also in *Urfaust* (19–20), that he had long since given up on the possibility of teaching others anything that would improve or convert them (372–73). This abdication of moral responsibility in scientific research may perhaps be understood psychologically as his reaction to the shock of having, as a young man, distributed poison in the name of medical science to thousands of human beings during a plague and then of having been praised for murdering them (1050–55). Whether that psychological explanation is valid or not, the separation of science from morality does form a dramaturgic key to his tragic character and may even be said to constitute his "tragic flaw" through which the denouement is shaped.[2] In this case, the denouement is not, as Mephistopheles had planned, Faust's damnation, but, as the Lord God had prophesied to Mephistopheles already in the Prologue in Heaven, his ultimate moral uprightness and his eventual salvation, because, the Lord explains, "even though he serves me now in a confused manner, I shall soon lead him into the light" (308–9). Therefore "a good man, even in his dark impulse, is always aware of the right path" (328–29). This divine "leading" along a path of which "a good man" is himself aware is the Goethean version of the age-old tension in many religions between the divine initiative and the human initiative in salvation, thus—in Augustinian theological terms—between grace and free will.[3]

But to complete that tension and to bring about that denouement, the tragic flaw must be combined with a redeeming virtue that continues to assert itself even in the depths of Faust's degrada-

1. Möbus 1964, 287–90 is an examination of this metaphor.
2. Aristotle *Poetics* 1453a–54b.
3. Loewenich 1959, 88–102.

tion and "dark impulse." That virtue is identified as "striving." For in the same address to Mephistopheles, the Lord God has characterized this as the source at once of human nobility and of human error: "As long as man strives, he also strays" (317).[4] At the outset of the drama Faust can speak of his striving as ebbing (696–98) and may recognize limits to that striving, declaring the sphere of the Easter faith to be beyond those bounds (767);[5] and yet he wishes that he could break out of them (1075). Nevertheless, although this striving is present in other species as well (912, 1098–99), it constitutes for him a special quality of the human spirit, over which the power of the devil seeks in vain to assert its dominance. As Faust taunts Mephistopheles, "You poor devil, what do you want to give? Has the spirit of a man in his sublime striving ever been comprehended by the likes of you?" (1675–77).[6] Yet, because what this devil promises to give him corresponds so precisely to this dimension of his personality, Faust can also assure Mephistopheles: "Just have no fear that I will break this contract! A striving with all my strength is precisely what I am promising" (1741–43). Even amid all the sensual allurements of the Classical Walpurgis Night, with its flashing "female limbs" (7283), the restless reaching and striving for still more and still higher asserts itself (7289–91). Therefore it is on the basis of this striving that his eventual salvation is attained (11934–37). Significantly, that salvation also represents the redemption of Faust's tragic flaw as a scientist; for now the one who had given up on the possibility of "teaching others anything that will improve and convert them" (372–73) is summoned to an eternity in which, as the Boy Souls sing, he "has learned, and he will teach" (12082–83). He will be able to teach the Boy Souls because he will also go on learning and because Gretchen herself will teach him. As she in her transfigured form prays in the last words that come from her in the drama, "Grant me that I may instruct him. This new day still dazzles him" (12092–93).[7]

4. Es irrt der Mensch, solang' er strebt.
5. Obenauer 1923, 122–23.
6. Molnár 1981, 56–59.
7. Vergönne mir, ihn zu belehren, / Noch blendet ihn der neue Tag.

It is also Faust's restless striving that eventually redeems and rescues his natural science. The three verbs in his original counsel of despair about the possibility that his science can "*teach* [lehren] others anything that will *improve* [bessern] and *convert* [bekehren] them" (372–73) belong together. For not only is he saved in order to engage in teaching, but in his natural science and his technology he has finally learned to regard the improvement of the human condition as an object of his striving that is both possible and desirable. Faust reaffirms that striving as the overriding trait of his spirit when he exclaims: "This globe of Earth still has room for great deeds. There are things in the offing that will be worthy of astonishment, and I can feel the energy for daring effort" (10181–84). He goes on to affirm his resolve to pit his energy and striving against those of the sea, which are going to waste in their natural state, and to triumph over them (10212–21).[8] But this titanic declaration of war and summons to victory is accompanied not by any explicit moral resolve to improve and convert others (372–73) but only by what, later in the nineteenth century, Nietzsche would call "the will to power." As Faust declares, "I will achieve dominion, property! The deed is everything, fame is nothing" (10187–88). Or, as Mephistopheles puts it, "Might makes right" (11184). Therefore, as long as it does not rise above this level, his striving remains, as Mephistopheles says cynically in the name of the entire demonic host, "an effort that is still supporting only our side" (11544); and "corrupted by great possessions and power, Faust is now a much more ruthless person than the young ruffian who stabbed Valentine to death and then abandoned Gretchen for the witches on the Brocken."[9]

The striving breaks out of this confinement and ruthlessness only when, at the very end, Faust the scientist and engineer finally begins to recognize his responsibility "to improve and convert others" (372–73). His technology has in fact been having that result concretely, well before Faust recognizes his responsibility

8. Examined by Heise 1982, 99–101.
9. Butler 1952, 261.

theoretically. Philemon describes to the Wanderer how the power of the sea has been domesticated, so that the force that had once "mishandled" him had now become "an image of Paradise" (11083–86). Thus Philemon and Baucis, together with the Wanderer who has returned to visit them, have been the beneficiaries of Faust's vast reclamation project. But as far as Faust himself is concerned, they are important for a different and contrary reason: it is their "humble cottage," together with "the crumbling chapel," that still "is not mine," so that his "vast estate is not unblemished" (11151–62). Thus he shows that "he hates their 'Hütte,' not just because it is a hindrance to his engineering plans, but because it is a reminder of his first great guilt."[10] This situation reminds Mephistopheles of King Ahab and Naboth's vineyard (11286–87).[11] As with the words of the temptation of Adam and Eve (in the Latin of the Vulgate of Genesis 3:5), "You shall be as God, knowing good and evil" (2048), and with the worship of the golden calf (5041), Mephistopheles seems to know his Bible better than Faust, whose science includes sacred philology (1220–37). Now "in extreme old age" (at 11143), according to a statement of Goethe to Eckermann "precisely a hundred years old,"[12] with enormous power and wealth, Faust still does not have enough. As he sighs, it "is the worst torture of all, to feel a lack when so little is lacking" (11251–52), namely, the cottage of these two old people. For in his self-centeredness he has not yet learned the fundamental social lesson of all morality, as this is formulated by his ally, the Emperor: that beyond "self-interest" there stand the higher claims of "gratitude, duty, and honor" (10393–96).[13]

All along there have nevertheless been anticipations of Faust's eventual moral development, and thus of his essential character as God's "servant" (299), who "serves [God] now, though in a con-

10. Wilkinson and Willoughby 1962, 106.
11. 1 Kings 21; Poggioli 1963, 3–24.
12. Eckermann, *Gespräche mit Goethe*, Part Two, 6 June 1831 (Bergemann 1987, 471).
13. Requadt 1964, 153–71, is a portrait of the figure of the Emperor.

fused way" (308). Already in the invocation of the Earth Spirit, he
expresses his readiness to bear not only the happiness of the world
but its sorrows (464–65). Solitary scholar though he is at the beginning of Part One, he finds, when he does go out into society and
associates with others, a source of joy and a way of knowing his real
humanity: "Here I can be free, here I am human!" (937–40.) In the
Study after coming in with the poodle, Faust finds another such
rare moment in which for a moment his "better self" takes control
and "unruliness and wild impulses subside, as thoughts of love
begin to stir—love of humanity, love of God" (1182–85), the "love
of humanity" and the "love of God" being closely linked with a
state in which "reason begins to speak again and hope revives"
(1198–99); but then comes the encounter with Mephistopheles.
The entire scene in the Forest Cavern represents such an anticipation even after that encounter, especially the apostrophe to the
Earth Spirit that opens it (3217–50). Similarly, when he is being
"catechized" by Margarete, he can assert his willingness to "surrender body and life for those I love," apparently referring not only
to her but to others (3419). Again, during the Classical Walpurgis
Night, Faust is clearly stirred by meeting Chiron, to whom he has
been directed as an authority (7209–13) and in whom he discovers
the combination of scientific and moral excellence that he has
hitherto found so elusive (7345–48). This encounter, too, seems to
anticipate, however faintly, the eventual dawn of conscience in
Faust's morality and theology, as does his vision, during the battle
of Part Two, Act IV, of a universal domesticity (9474) extending all
the way to "Europe's furthest mountains" (9513). Nevertheless, all
of this is a combination, and a social and moral lesson, that Doctor
Faust, natural scientist and theologian though he is, really learns
and completely takes to heart only in the hour of his death.

Of Faust's many soliloquies, the one that marks that hour of
death is in many respects the most remarkable. There appear four
gray sisters—Lack [Mangel], Guilt [Schuld], Care [Sorge], and
Need [Not]—followed at a distance by their brother, Death [Tod];
"the connection of Care with Mephistopheles, who is himself the
persistent attack of nothingness upon the unity of the person with

itself, remains unexpressed, but it is more than evident in the successive stages of actions that underlie this writing."[14] Faust is struck blind by Care,[15] but he is still striving and pressing forward with his ambitious project. He promises "the loveliest reward" for "strict discipline and rapid but industrious work," because "to complete a great project one mind is enough for a thousand hands" (11507–10), the "one mind," of course, being Faust's and the "thousand hands" being those of his menial laborers. For his social outlook, too, is still one of regarding other human beings as a means to his own ends, "setting a boundary to the waves and surrounding the sea with a strict curb" (11540–43)—when, by yet another irony, what they are in fact digging with those shovels is his grave. But finally, because in his blindness he is being brightly illumined from within (11500), the truth begins to dawn on him "with a clear mind," as the Spirit Chorus had urged near the beginning of the drama (1624), that the zenith of his natural science and technology will not be mere self-aggrandizement but rather "opening up living space for millions to live, not in security, but in free activity" (11562–64). This soliloquy presents a complex picture of the relation between technology and society.[16] For now Faust has learned, contrary to his original complaint (1067), that his scientific knowledge can be useful and his technology constructive, when it is placed into the service of others and when it enables them to be free. As one Goethe scholar has said with a characteristic combination of insight and irony, Goethe "found no more fitting symbol for Faust's renunciation of magic than this assuming the position of a welfare engineer."[17] Blind though he is, Faust now can see what he has just called "the mob" (11540) for what it truly is, a "free people" standing on a "free soil" (11579–80).[18] For, as he summarizes here, "This is the ultimate conclusion of wisdom: the only person who deserves either freedom or life is the one who has to

14. Kommerell 1944, 108.
15. Burdach 1923, 1–60; Michelsen 1962, 26–35.
16. Mieth 1980, 90–102.
17. E. Heller 1966, 43.
18. It is useful to consult the comments of Wild 1991, 122–27.

win it anew every day" (11574–76). And now, having agreed in his original deal with Mephistopheles, "If ever I say to any moment, 'Bide a while! You are so beautiful!' then you can put me in shackles and I will gladly surrender" (1699–1702), he is finally ready at this moment to say just that: "To this moment I would be willing to say, 'Bide a while! You are so beautiful!' . . . In anticipation of such sublime happiness, I now enjoy the supreme moment" (11581–86).[19] With those words he dies, free at last to know Nature and to be one with Nature in eternity, something that the spirits of Mephistopheles had promised in their first song to Faust, with its talk of an ethereal blue sky and noble stones (1447–1505), but that Mephistopheles could never deliver. Thus his death, in an ironic way, may be seen as carrying out the prophecy of Lynkeus to him earlier in this final act: "Fortune salutes you at this supreme moment!" (11150).

For the attitude of Mephistopheles toward Faust as natural scientist and Faust as pantheist, epitomized by the devil's interest only in the What and not in the How (11185), is itself an intimation, and ultimately becomes a provocation, of this moral outcome. Even while tempting Faust to accept his bargain early in Part One, Mephistopheles solemnly discourages him from his pantheistic yearnings. "Believe me," he warns, "this Whole is made only for a God! He dwells in eternal light."[20] God had cast the devils into darkness and had placed humanity between that light and that darkness (1780–84). Late in Part Two, Mephistopheles supposes that he can manipulate Faust's natural science, and specifically his reclamation of land from the sea, to his own nihilistic advantage, because, he explains, "the elements are in league with us" (11546–50).[21] But in the event, "on the detour of an apparent overpowering of reality with the help of magic and of the collapse of this effort, Faust finds the path into his own depths and ultimately the path to his very own transcendent destiny, a path that would never have

19. The changes in the final version of these lines are documented in Dietze 1975, 14–18.

20. 1 Tim. 6:16.

21. Hohlfeld 1936, 285–86.

been opened up for him without that detour and without that all-consuming energy."[22] Taking advantage of Faust's satiety with scientific research and with rationality, Mephistopheles has used it, in his declaratory aria, to repudiate all rationality and all science (1851–55). But it should have been clear from the outset that truly to "have" Faust, and to have him "for sure," as he promises himself in that aria, would be impossible to anyone who did not and could not in some profound way share his reverence for Nature.

Already in the Prologue in Heaven, Mephistopheles, echoing the cosmic song of the three archangels (267–70), makes it obvious that he does not share their celebration of the cosmos: "About the sun and other worlds I have nothing to say. All I can see is how human beings make themselves miserable. The little god of this world goes right on as always, and is as strange as he was on the first day" (279–82). Almost enviously, he delineates the difference between himself and human beings, who "feel the mysterious activity of an eternally reigning Nature" (4985–86) when he does not even know how to hum (7175)—although in the scene in Auerbach's Cellar in Leipzig he does manage to sing a little (2211–18, 2223–38). Therefore, when Faust celebrates spring's coming and concludes with a description of how this can influence human beings in their physical existence (3841–47), Mephistopheles must admit that this is all quite alien to him, because "for me it is always wintry in my body, and I would want to have snow and frost surrounding me" (3848–50). Much later, when Mephistopheles has expounded his own understanding of natural science and claimed that he was present at the creation, Faust finds it "noteworthy to observe how devils look upon Nature." But Mephistopheles again admits: "What do I care? Let Nature be as it may!" (10122–24). It is that view that underlies what has been called "Mephisto's way of getting into Nature."[23]

In their original negotiations Mephistopheles promised that Faust would be "released and set free" (1542). But now it is a declaration of independence from Mephistopheles and from the

22. Petsch 1926a, 171.
23. D. Lohmeyer 1975, 225–35.

devil's attitude toward Nature when, in the land reclamation project, Faust the natural scientist recovers his humanity and his authentic freedom—or rather, finds it fully for the first time. With this freedom he also discovers an eternity that he had summarily dismissed. Already when Mephistopheles makes his initial stipulation, "I will bind myself to your service *here* and will be at your disposal, without relief or respite. If we meet *beyond,* you shall do the same for me" (1656–59), Faust replies with bravado: "The beyond does not bother me very much. If you ever shatter this world to bits, then let the other come. My pleasures spring forth from this Earth. . . . I do not want to listen to whether people in that future will hate and love, or whether in those spheres there may be top or bottom" (1660–70).[24] Later he reinforces this hedonistic argument in the name of a scientific thisworldiness, for which "this globe of Earth" is all-sufficient and "eternity" is of no consequence (11441–47). But at the end, in the eternal world he has now discovered, there lies the hope of an immortality somehow transcending the here and now with the assurance: "My days on the Earth will not disappear in the aeons without a trace" (11583–84).[25] With the transcendence over space and time also comes, paradoxically, that unity with the All, within both space and time, for which Faust as pantheist has longed.

Similarly, not only the natural scientist as pantheist but also the poetic artist as polytheist stands in a developmental but dialectical relation to the moral philosopher as monotheist, and the declaration of independence from Mephistopheles likewise entails a rescue from the thrall of sorcery that attends polytheism. For the polytheism of Doctor Faust finds its eventual poetic expression in aesthetics, as embodied above all in Helen of Troy; but the aestheticism, in turn, climaxes in a break with sorcery and a *Götterdämmerung* that may be more gentle, but is no less comprehensive, than the more familiar one with which Richard Wagner's *Der*

24. On the relation between the here and now and the beyond in this negotiation, Burghold 1913, 64–82; also Schultz 1928, 288–309, and H. Scholz 1934.

25. Kühnemann 1938, 16–19.

Ring des Nibelungen concludes. And like the reclamation of land from the sea, the *Götterdämmerung* sets the stage for Faust to move to—or, at any rate, toward—the "mode of thought" of moral philosopher as monotheist and thus toward eventual salvation. When Faust reappears as knight, poet, and priest in Act III of Part Two, after an interval that is measured in the drama by 1700 lines,[26] the leader of the chorus, addressing herself to the divine Helen of Troy, celebrates his return in the classic strophes of a polytheistic hymn:

> Unless it has been only for a brief time that the gods, as is their wont, have temporarily lent this man a wondrous figure, sublime demeanor, and agreeable presence, then everything he undertakes will be successful, whether in battle against men or in the gentler warfare with the most beautiful women. He is certainly preferable to many whom I have seen with my own eyes who had a high reputation. Now I see the Prince as he advances reverently, with slow and solemn step. O Queen, turn toward him! (9182–91).[27]

Although the favor of the gods is so notoriously fickle, this choral prayer finds in Faust a special combination of exalted aesthetic qualities ("a wondrous figure") and transcendent moral qualities ("sublime demeanor")—a combination long since epitomized in his own language about "the Good and the Beautiful," with its echoes of the classical Greek *kalokagathia* (1207).

From the perspective of conventional morality, however, it is downright offensive that such a combination of moral and aesthetic qualities should be described in a hymn addressed to, of all beings, Helen of Troy. At her first appearance, an envious woman dismisses her as damaged goods that have "passed through many hands" (6528–29). But it is not only such prudes who are quick to

26. On the significance of Faust's silences, Victor Lange in Wilkinson 1984, 133–52.

27. Wenn diesem nicht die Götter, wie sie öfter tun, / Für wenige Zeit nur wundernswürdige Gestalt, / Erhabnen Anstand, liebenswerte Gegenwart / Vorübergänglich liehen, wird ihm jedesmal, / Was er beginnt, gelingen, sei's in Männerschlacht, / So auch im kleinen Kriege mit den schönsten Fraun. / Er ist fürwahr gar vielen andern vorzuziehn, / Die ich doch auch als hochgeschätzt mit Augen sah. / Mit langsam-ernstem, ehrfurchtsvoll gehaltnem Schritt / Seh' ich den Fürsten; wende dich, o Königin!

point to the ambiguity of aestheticism. Helen herself bemoans the "iron fate" of being so beautiful that men make fools of themselves over her and spare nothing in their passion to possess her. This is, she continues, a fate that seems especially to affect polytheism, as "demigods, heroes, gods, and even demons" have "abducted and seduced" her and dragged her from one place to another (9247–53). In her last farewell to Faust, that theme of fate and beauty, so closely tied to poetic polytheism, sounds with an even greater desperation: "The old adage that beauty and happiness are ultimately incompatible is, alas, being vindicated in me. The bonds of life and of love are torn asunder. Lamenting them both, I bid you a painful farewell and throw myself into your arms for the last time."[28] The stage directions add: "She embraces Faust. All that is bodily about her disappears, and her dress and veil remain in his arms" (9939–44).

In spite of that ambiguity, the beauty that Helen embodies, that the poetic artist celebrates, and that the polytheist worships truly is divine, also in the ultimate sense, as Mephistopheles seems to admit (6315–16). It is not only in pagan Greek mythology that the creation of Earth is described as the work of an artist (7550–57). Already in the Prologue in Heaven, the Lord God himself turns to his beloved angels with the charge to "rejoice in the beauty that is living and rich" and to be embraced in love by "that which is becoming, that which is eternally active and living," so that "with their continuing thoughts" they might give solidity to "that which floats in shifting appearances" (344–49),[29] "thoughts" that become truly "solid" for Faust, together with all that is noble and beautiful, only at the other end of the drama (12104–11). For that reason, the pathetic plea of Lynkeus—the legendary watchman

28. Ein altes Wort bewährt sich leider auch an mir: / Daß Glück und Schönheit dauerhaft sich nicht vereint. / Zerrissen ist des Lebens wie der Liebe Band; / Bejammernd beide, sag' ich schmerzlich Lebewohl / Und werfe mich noch einmal in die Arme dir.

29. Doch ihr, die echten Göttersöhne, / Erfreut euch der lebendig reichen Schöne! / Das Werdende, das ewig wirkt und lebt, / Umfass' euch mit der Liebe holden Schranken, / Und was in schwankender Erscheinung schwebt, / Befestiget mit dauernden Gedanken.

who could see through stone, "Lynkeus the sharp-eyed, who brought the sacred ship by night and day past rocks and beaches" (7377–78), but who in this case neglected his duty because he was smitten by Helen's beauty—does have a certain validity even beyond the boundaries of his own polytheism: "I forgot the duties of the watchman, and completely forgot the horn I was sworn to blow. Only threaten to destroy me—but Beauty restrains all wrath" (9242–45),[30] because Beauty seems able to restrain even the wrath of the one true God. The absoluteness of the Beautiful bears a profound affinity to the absoluteness of monotheism in another and rather surprising respect. As the events of the Classical Walpurgis Night make evident (7873–76), it is characteristic of polytheism that it splits up the Divine into many supernatural beings, who engage in rivalry, competition, and mutual ridicule (8190–91). By contrast, aestheticism, like monotheism, demands a total and undivided allegiance; for "Beauty is indivisible, and whoever has wholly possessed it would sooner destroy it with a curse than share it" (9061–62). But the gods of polytheism become one only through aesthetics, when they are united by revelation through the poetic artist, as the Prologue on the Stage has already announced (156–57). And therefore when the gods of polytheism have disappeared into the twilight, it is the poets who abide (9955–59).

Polytheistic though it may be, Faust's aestheticism is no less alien to the devil than is Faust's pantheistic yearning for the All (1780–84), and there can be no elevation of both pantheism and polytheism to monotheism until Faust learns this about Mephistopheles and takes fundamental offense at it. It is to be expected that a Catholic Archbishop (10981–84), and at his behest a Catholic Emperor (11003–4), should be offended at mighty deeds that have been made possible through being in league with the devil, or that a simple and superstitious peasant woman like Baucis should object to such deeds on the grounds that "this whole business was simply

30. Ich vergaß des Wächters Pflichten, / Völlig das beschworne Horn; / Drohe nur, mich zu vernichten— / Schönheit bändigt allen Zorn.
On Lynkeus, Samson Eitrem in Pauly-Wissowa 1893–1963, 13:2470.

not right" (11113–14). But Helen of Troy, too, penetrates the Phorcyad disguise of Mephistopheles (9072–73). Above all, it is Margarete, the "angel filled with intuition" as Faust calls her (3494), who gives voice to the offense and downright horror that are always the only appropriate reaction to Mephistopheles (and should have been Faust's reaction to him from the beginning), and he reciprocates by recognizing in her his most dangerous opponent. Even as she is dying, in the closing scene of Part One, she cries out to Faust in delirious terror: "What is that rising out of the ground? That one! That one! Send him away! What does he want in this sacred place? He wants me!" (4601–4).[31] But she has reacted this way to him all along: "He overwhelms me so completely that whenever he comes up to us, I get the feeling that I don't love you any more, and when he is present, that I can't pray any more," she says in *Urfaust* (1187–90).[32] Or, as she says in Part One of *Faust*, in the strongest language she uses anywhere about anyone or anything, either in *Urfaust* or in *Faust*, "Nothing in my life has ever stabbed my heart the way that man's revolting face does. . . . His very presence makes my blood boil. Otherwise I have a positive reaction to everyone. But as much as I yearn to see you, I have a mysterious dread of that man" (3473–80).[33] When she adds piously, "May God forgive me if I am doing him an injustice!" (3482) and when Faust interposes condescendingly, "Baby Doll, don't be afraid of him!" (3476), it is evident that in her naive piety she sees into the demonic more accurately than does Doctor Faust with all his learned sophistication about both science and theology. His defiant boast, "I am not plagued by either scruples or doubts, and I am not afraid of either hell or the devil" (368–69), finds its appropriate gloss in the words of Mephistopheles after a witch has

31. Was steigt aus dem Boden herauf? / Der! der! Schick' ihn fort! / Was will der an dem heiligen Ort? / Er will mich!

32. Das übermannt mich so sehr, / Daß, wo er mag zu uns treten, / Mein ich sogar, ich liebte dich nicht mehr. / Auch, wenn er da ist, könnt ich nimmer beten.

33. Es hat mir in meinem Leben / So nichts einen Stich ins Herz gegeben, / Als des Menschen widrig Gesicht. . . . / Seine Gegenwart bewegt mir das Blut. / Ich bin sonst allen Menschen gut; / Aber wie ich mich sehne, dich zu schauen, / Hab ich vor dem Menschen ein heimlich Grauen.

referred to "Esquire Satan [Junker Satan]": "All of that has long since been inscribed in the book of fable. But men are no better off because of that. They are rid of the Evil One, but the evil ones remain" (2507–9), which is, as was observed a century ago, "a side thrust at the Age of Enlightenment."[34] Such a lack of acknowledgment does not bother Mephistopheles at all; as he reminds Faust, "the common people are not aware of the devil even when he grabs them by the collar" (2181–82), because the devil does not need to be believed in or even to be recognized in order to exercise his power. Faust, however, does have to recognize him for what he is if he is ever to get free of that power. The banter between Faust and Mephistopheles throughout the drama is, in this respect, a major part of the seriously intended jests, but only gradually does the total chasm between their two world views become obvious. Faust knows all along, as he says in response to the devil's initial offer, that "the devil is an egotist and is not likely to do for God's sake what is useful to someone else" (1651–53). Even female beauty does not appeal to Mephistopheles (11799–800),[35] who is disgusted by the human body (1355–58); and he admits that he could never be content with only one woman, regardless of how beautiful she is (10170–75).

Though it is spoken by Megaera, it is a Mephistophelian parody of Faust's constant "striving" to observe that as soon as someone has his arms around the object of his passion he begins to yearn for another (5373–75). The vision of Helen of Troy sharpens this contrast between Faust and Mephistopheles. Faust is overwhelmed by the vision: "The most beautiful image of a woman! Is it possible, can the woman be that beautiful? Must I see in this reclining body the sum total of all the heavens? Can anything like this exist on earth?" (2436–40).[36] The response of Mephistopheles is yet another of the seriously intended jests: "Of course, if a God labors

34. C. Thomas 1892–97, 1:306; on the controversy over the place of the concept of "evil" in *Faust,* Mason 1964, 7–11.

35. Powell 1970, 113–14.

36. Das schönste Bild von einem Weibe! / Ist's möglich, ist das Weib so schön? / Muß ich an diesem hingestreckten Leibe / Den Inbegriff von allen Himmeln sehn? / So etwas findet sich auf Erden?

mightily for six whole days and himself says 'Hurrah' at the end, something clever has to come of it" (2441–43). When Helen of Troy first appears in person, thanks to his gift to Faust of the powers of sorcery, he recognizes her but shrugs her off as "pretty enough, I suppose," but not for him (6479–80). Even in the sensuality that he has been abetting by calling up Helen, he does not share, in fact does not even understand, Faust's deepest yearnings as poetic artist and polytheist any more than he does Faust's deepest intuitions as natural scientist and pantheist.

For in fundamental opposition to either pantheism or polytheism, it is the metaphysical nihilism of Mephistopheles that sets him apart from Faust.[37] Though he is deep into the pact with the devil, Faust is able, in an exchange with Gretchen, to formulate his pantheistic credo (3432–45). But the devil's own credo, formulated during the negotiations over the pact, is nihilism: "I am the spirit that constantly negates! And rightly so, for everything that comes into existence is fit only to go out of existence, and it would be better if nothing ever got started in the first place. Thus all that you call sin, destruction—evil, in short—is my proper element" (1338–44).[38] When the pact appears to have reached its consummation, with Faust's death and his recitation of the fateful formula, "Bide a while, you are so beautiful!" (11582), it is that "proper element" of nihilism that asserts itself in similar language. While the chorus sings, "It is over," Mephistopheles, although he himself has spoken of Faust's death "with this, not accidental, echo of Christ's end," namely, "It is finished [Es ist vollbracht],"[39] goes on to sneer: "Over! A stupid word. Why 'over'? Over or pure nothingness—they are exactly the same! What is the point of this eternal creating! To drag what is created back to nothingness! 'It is over!' What does it amount to? It is no better than if it had never

37. On "Teufelsnihilismus," there are astute comments in Mann 1968, 306–12.

38. Ich bin der Geist, der stets verneint! / Und das mit Recht; denn alles, was entsteht, / Ist wert, daß es zugrunde geht; / Denn besser wär's, daß nichts entstünde. / So ist denn alles, was ihr Sünde, / Zerstörung, kurz das Böse nennt, / Mein eigentliches Element.

39. 11594, quoting John 19:30; Emrich 1957, 403.

existed at all, and yet it comes full circle as though it did have existence. I would rather have eternal emptiness instead" (11595–11603).[40]

Throughout, Mephistopheles is always on the lookout for something on which to pronounce his nihilistic curse (2805–6). In this nihilistic Mephistophelian universe, everything is inverted. Not only does might make right; it even invokes a kind of demonic trinity of "war, commerce, and piracy, three in one and inseparable," as the creeds of the church said about Father, Son, and Holy Spirit (11184–88). According to the Judeo-Christian tradition, Mephistopheles and all the satanic host are fallen angels, created holy but cast out of heaven for their disobedience; but this, too, is reversed here, so that the holy angels become "devils, but in disguise" (11696).

It is in the context of that nihilism that we should read the striking exchange between them, when Mephistopheles describes the strange new world into which they are entering together, where all the distances are "eternally empty," where Faust will not hear his own footsteps, and where there will be no place to rest (6246–48). Faust is still bantering, labeling Mephistopheles "the first of all the mystagogues who ever misled his faithful neophytes, but in an inverted way: You send me into emptiness, so that I can improve my art and my powers" (6249–52). Yet he is also still probing, because "in your Nothingness I hope to find the All" (6255–56). Thus Faust seems intent on turning even the nihilism of Mephistopheles to his purposes, both the scientific-pantheistic purpose ("the All") and the aesthetic-polytheistic purpose ("my art and my powers"). This path leads, however, not to the "All" of Faust but to the "Nothingness" of Mephistopheles, as Faust begins to see when he labels what Mephistopheles calls "military tactics" for what it truly is: "Deception! Sorcerer's tricks! Utter trickery!"

40. Vorbei! Ein dummes Wort. / Warum vorbei? / Vorbei und reines Nicht, vollkommnes Einerlei! / Was soll uns denn das ew'ge Schaffen! / Geschaffenes zu nichts hinwegzuraffen! / "Da ist's vorbei!" Was ist daran zu lesen? / Es ist so gut, als wär' es nicht gewesen, / Und treibt sich doch im Kreis, als wenn es wäre. / Ich liebte mir dafür das Ewig-Leere.

(10300–10301)—made all the more ironic by the singing of the traditional Christian hymn, *Te Deum laudamus,* in thanks for the military victory (10863–66).

Just as the first signal of Faust's entry into the nihilistic world of Mephistopheles was the preoccupation with the black arts, so it is his decisive break with sorcery that marks his exit from that world into the world of freedom and of authentic humanity, of morality and ultimately of monotheism. An exclamation of Panthalis, a polytheist, after the departure of her queen, Helen of Troy, which equates "sorcery" with "a desolate spiritual duress" (9962–63), seeks to deliver polytheism from its darker side.[41] In response to her, the spirits celebrate their deliverance, as they are "returned to the daylight" and restored to unity with an "eternally living Nature" (9985–89). At first Faust's sorcery may seem playful, as he sports with the poodle (1238–58) and bars the exit to Mephistopheles by the use of the pentagram (1395–96). Then his sorcery confers on him various supernatural powers, summoning Helen of Troy and transporting him "miraculously to Greece" (7074). And, in response to his command to Mephistopheles to carry out his demand as the devil had promised to do (10233), sorcery grants him success in what one interpreter has called his "grandiose vision" (11109–14, 11131–34).[42] Eventually, however, Faust finds that, in the words of the Sorcerer's Apprentice in Goethe's familiar ballad of 1797, he "cannot now get rid of the spirits whom [he has] summoned." Those words seem to be echoed in Faust's response to Care, "Demons, I know, are hard to get rid of" (11491–92), the words "I know" suggesting that by now he has begun to know this very well.

For not only does he tell himself, "Do not pronounce any formulas of sorcery" (11423); but in a prayer to Nature, which Goethe wrote in April or May 1831,[43] Faust has just cried out desperately for deliverance from sorcery and its dark powers: "If I

41. As Münzhuber 1947, 13, observes, it is "especially since the relationship with Helen that Mephistopheles stands over against Faust with a constantly increasing lack of understanding."

42. Obenauer 1922, 140.

43. Landeck 1981, 111, 216; also Bluhm 1966, 8–26.

could only put magic far out of my path, utterly unlearn the
formulas of sorcery, and stand in thy presence, O Nature, just as a
man, that would make it worthwhile to be a human being"
(11404–7).[44] This anguished cry, as "the most paradoxical echo
and answer to the wager,"[45] takes him back in memory to the days
before his satiety brought him into the devil's power, and before he
cursed everything good and holy (1583–1606). "That is what I was
once upon a time," he recalls, "before I explored the realm of
darkness and, with my sacrilegious words, brought this curse upon
myself and upon the world" (11408–9). He has brought down this
curse of superstition on the natural world, on human reason, on day
and night: "Now the air is so filled with such spookiness that no one
knows how to avoid it. Even if a day smiles upon us with its
rationality, the night tangles us up in a web of dreams. We come
home happy from the fields in springtime. A bird croaks. What
does it croak? Calamity! We are surrounded on all sides by superstition, events of omen, portent, warning. And so we stand, all alone
with our terror" (11410–18).[46]

Now the one who is speaking seems to be not Goethe's sorcerer's apprentice but Shakespeare's sorcerer, Prospero in *The Tempest,* the play that is the source for the figure of Ariel who has
appeared near the end of Part One (4239–42) and at the beginning
of Part Two (4613–78): "This rough magic / I here abjure," as he
casts his magic wand and book of witchcraft into the sea.[47] But
because "magic in its turn is a binding of nature," as Northrop Frye

44. Könnt' ich Magie von meinem Pfad entfernen, / Die Zaubersprüche
ganz und gar verlernen, / Stünd' ich, Natur, vor dir ein Mann allein, / Da wär's
der Mühe wert, ein Mensch zu sein.
The comments of K. Thomas 1971, 469–501, are appropriate also here.
45. Balthasar 1947, 510.
46. Nun ist die Luft von solchem Spuk so voll, / Daß niemand weiß, wie er
ihn meiden soll. / Wenn auch ein Tag uns klar vernünftig lacht, / Im Traum-
gespinst verwickelt uns die Nacht; / Wir kehren froh von junger Flur
zurück, / Ein Vogel krächzt; was krächzt er? Mißgeschick. / Von Aberglauben
früh und spat umgarnt: / Es eignet sich, es zeigt sich an, es warnt. / Und so
verschüchtert, stehen wir allein.
47. William Shakespeare, *The Tempest,* Act V, Scene 1, lines 50–51; on some
relations between *The Tempest* and *Faust,* observations by Boyd 1932, 56–59, and
Hamlin 1976, 144 n. 1.

once noted, it follows that "the speech in which Prospero [as well as Faust] renounces his magic represents the release of nature as well."[48]

Such sorcery and such polytheism stand in stark opposition not only to the pantheistic religion of Nature but to traditional monotheism and Christian orthodoxy, as Part Two, Act IV, makes clear in a scene of considerable irony. "It is with bitter pain," the Archbishop admonishes the Emperor, "that I find you in league with Satan." This is, he continues, "a blasphemy before the Lord God and before the Pope, the Holy Father" (10981–84). The Emperor is "terrified by the gravity of [his] error" and heeds the admonition, in repentance before God and in submission to the authority of the church (11003). But perhaps the simplest—and the starkest— expression of this opposition between sorcery and the Christian tradition comes from old Philemon, who, after narrating the story of Faust's sorcery to his guest, the Wanderer, exhorts: "Let us go over to the chapel, to catch the final light of the sun. Let us toll the bell, kneel, pray—and place our trust in the old God!" (11139– 42).[49] This "old God" had permitted the sea to rage, whereas the sorcery of the "new god" has now replaced that raging sea with "a garden" and "an image of Paradise" (11082–11106); nonetheless it continues to be in the "old God" that Philemon wants to repose his trust. By far the most complete expression of the opposition is embodied in Gretchen, whose statement of revulsion at Mephistopheles, discussed earlier in this chapter, comes right after she has accused Faust of having rejected Christianity (3468). Both the accusation and the revulsion are altogether in keeping with her character, as this is manifested throughout Part One. She first appears on her way from church, and, as Mephistopheles puts it contemptuously after having spied on her, "she came from her priest, who pronounced absolution on her from every sin" (2621– 22). Her mother's churchy piety is of the same sort, Mephistopheles goes on to explain in the identical tone, because "that woman has

48. Frye 1986, 180.

49. Laßt uns zur Kapelle treten, / Letzten Sonnenblick zu schaun! / Laßt uns läuten, knieen, beten / Und dem alten Gott vertraun!

an excellent sense of smell," by which she can tell "whether something is sacred or profane" (2817–20). After Gretchen has fallen, his demonic colleague, the Evil Spirit, finding her in the cathedral, taunts her about her childish devotion (3776–82).

When Faust, with the help of Mephistopheles, has sneaked into Gretchen's bedchamber in her absence, it is likewise Gretchen as a devout child that comes to his imagination (2699–2701). Her old-fashioned piety has given her the modest manner and attitude that Faust finds so irresistible (3169–79). And therefore, after his importuning has also proved to be irresistible and Gretchen the seduced is imprisoned while Faust the seducer remains at liberty, she turns yet again to her churchly religiosity. This now expresses itself in the sacrament of penance, but also in the invocation of the saints, as in prison she, the monotheist, urges him, the pantheist-polytheist, to "kneel down together and pray to the saints" (4453) and as she herself prays in her fervent petition to the Virgin Mary (3588–95). Although it is colored by his self-centeredness, Faust does seem to have some sense of what he is confronting in her faith, more sense of it at any rate than Mephistopheles does, and he chides the devil for his blindness to it: "You monster," he exclaims. "You do not grasp how this loyal and dear soul, filled with a faith that is for her the sole way to salvation, is experiencing holy terror at the thought that she must regard as lost the man she loves the most" (3528–33)[50]—thus seemingly attributing to this pious Roman Catholic soul the Lutheran doctrine of salvation by faith alone.[51] And therefore, after her arrest, the burning of the eternal light in the Catholic sacristy represents to him the contrast between her and the darkness within himself, as he describes it to Mephistopheles (3650–54). The contrast adds to the poignancy of her impassioned outburst to him about his alienation from Christianity (3468), and to the condescension voiced in the explanation by Mephistopheles that "girls are always very interested in whether

50. Du Ungeheuer siehst nicht ein, / Wie diese treue liebe Seele / Von ihrem Glauben voll, / Der ganz allein / Ihr selig machend ist, sich heilig quäle, / Daß sie den liebsten Mann verloren halten soll.

51. Jarras 1969 is a brief but thoughtful discussion of these issues.

someone is devout and simple according to traditional custom"
(3525–26), which appears also in *Urfaust* (1217–18). The one com-
ponent of this churchly Christianity that she singles out is the
doctrine of the sacraments.[52] "You do not respect the holy sacraments," she charges Faust. And when he retorts, "But I do honor
them," she rejoins that he honors them "without any yearning for
them" and that he has not gone to Mass or to confession for a long
time (3422–25). Faust unwittingly confirms Margarete's charge of
indifference to the sacraments when he says lightheartedly a bit
earlier that he "envies the body of the Lord when her lips touch it"
in receiving Holy Communion (3334–35), whereas for her it is
natural to promise to pray Requiem Masses at the death even of
someone she has never known personally (2942). To Faust, when
people come out of Mass into the spring sunshine, this means that
"they have all been brought out of the solemn darkness of the
churches into the light" (927–28), because the church is benighted
and true enlightenment derives from Nature.

Yet it seems clear that he has not always been so indifferent to
the faith of the church and to its sacraments. He speaks wistfully of
his early days, when "the love of heaven stooped down to kiss me in
the solemn silence of the Sabbath" (771–72). Although he is now a
person in whom "faith is absent" (765) and who pronounces a curse
on faith, hope, and charity (1604–5), there was, he claims, a time
when he was "rich in hope and firm in faith" (1026). He interprets
it as a vestigial remnant, albeit a deceitful one, of that early time
that he did not go through with his impulse to commit suicide
(1583–86).[53] It may be another such remnant when in his confusion and doubt he speaks of yearning for divine revelation, "which
does not shine more worthily and more beautifully than in the New
Testament," only to experience further confusion as he tries to find
the right way to translate "the sacred original into my beloved
German" when it speaks of the divine Logos in the opening words
of the Gospel of John (1216–37).

52. Meinhold 1958, 148–49, 249–51.
53. Wenn aus dem schrecklichen Gewühle / Ein süß bekannter Ton mich
zog, / Den Rest von kindlichem Gefühle / Mit Anklang froher Zeit betrog.

Prominent in Faust's reminiscences of the lost faith of his childhood is its penitential dimension, when he had "tormented himself with praying and with fasting . . . with tears and sighs and wringing of hands" (1025–27). Although penance has been the subject of several "jests" at various stages of the poem, some though not all of them coming from Mephistopheles,[54] they, too, turn out to have been in some sense "seriously intended"; for it is this same penitential dimension, now in Gretchen's Catholicism, so simple yet so profound, that saves her—and that finally, through her, saves Faust himself. Her mother's piety was focused on the sacrament of penance; thus Marthe warns Margarete that if her mother were to find out about the jewel box she has found in her room, she would rush to the confessional with it (2879–80). Following her mother's example, Margarete herself is constantly going to confession even though she has nothing to confess (2624–25). When their friend Barbara becomes pregnant out of wedlock, their mutual friend Lieschen tells Margarete that now Barbara will have to appear in church in penitential garb (3568–69). Therefore, after the same fate has befallen Margarete, Valentin, her brother, threatens her with the same penitential discipline and with excommunication from the sacraments (3756–57). In the church, not only the taunting of the Evil Spirit (3776–82) but the contrition in her own conscience oppresses her, so that even the organ music is stifling (3808–12). When her end comes, therefore, at the conclusion of Part One, she surrenders herself in penance, crying out, "The judgment of God! To thee have I submitted myself!" (4605) and "Father, I am thine! Save me! You angels, you heavenly hosts, encamp around me to preserve me!" (4607–9).[55] Mephistopheles pronounces her damned, "Sie ist gerichtet! [She is judged!]." That would be in keeping with the traditional versions of the story, in which "Judicatus est!" is the verdict on Faust at the end.[56] But

54. See, for example, 2624–25, 2834–40, 10991–92.
55. Gericht Gottes! dir hab' ich mich übergeben! . . . / Dein bin ich, Vater! Rette mich! / Ihr Engel! Ihr heiligen Scharen, / Lagert euch umher, mich zu bewahren!
The closing words are an allusion to Ps. 34:7.
56. Hamlin 1976, 117 n. 5.

here, in what has been called "the only instance of gratuitous supernatural intervention in the action of the tragedy between the moment when the curtain first rises on the figure of Faust in his study and the moment of Faust's death,"[57] a voice from heaven dramatically corrects Mephistopheles (and corrects the version at the conclusion of *Urfaust*) by changing a couple of letters: "Ist ger*et*tet! [She is saved!]" (4611). This comes as a response to her desperate plea for her child (whether directed to God or to Faust), "Rette! rette!" (4562) and then definitely to God alone, "Rette mich!" (4607).

Thus when Faust's own end comes, at the conclusion of Part Two, once more penance brings salvation, and with the same dramatic word, "gerettet" (11934). As one commentator has pointed out, "Only divine judgment can determine this, and if—as the advent of the angels proves—it decides in Faust's favor, despite the heavy guilt that rests on him, it represents a justice tempered by mercy and love."[58] It is important to note, however, that the repentance over this "heavy guilt" is not unambiguously attributed to Faust himself. The closing plea of Doctor Marianus is addressed to "all who have been made tender through repentance" (12097), which apparently, "like everything else here, applies to Faust, too."[59] Significantly, there have been in earlier scenes only very indirect references to any repentance on his part, as when, in the opening scene of Part Two, Act I, directly after the death of Gretchen, Ariel has told the elves attending Faust to "ease the dire conflict in the man's heart, pluck out the bitter burning arrows of reproach, purge his soul of horror" (4623–25).[60] Now, near the finale, in Act V of Part Two, Faust's words about deeds that had been "commanded quickly and done too quickly" (11382) did seem to bespeak regret or even remorse, if not quite repentance; but then they were followed almost immediately by the statement of Guilt,

---

57. Atkins 1953, 433.

58. Hohlfeld 1921, 534; the comments of H. Jaeger 1950, 109–52, are also pertinent here.

59. Trunz 1968, 636.

60. Besänftiget des Herzens grimmen Strauß, / Entfernt des Vorwurfs glühend bittre Pfeile, / Sein Innres reinigt von erlebtem Graus.

one of the four gray sisters, "There I amount to nothing" (11388). In this final scene, bearing the appellation "The One Woman Penitent, Formerly Called Gretchen" (at 12084), Margarete plays her part, but penance is a pervading theme throughout it. It is to penance, "those roses from the hands of the loving and holy women penitents," that the Younger Angels attribute their "victory" and conquest over the demonic kingdom and their "rescue of the treasure of this soul"—Faust (11942–53).[61] When, therefore, the Heavenly Host at Faust's burial intones the theme of "granting forgiveness to sinners, granting life to dust" (11679–80),[62] or when, on the same occasion, the Chorus of Angels affirms that those who have "damned themselves" may have the hope of "joyfully redeeming themselves from evil" through the healing power of truth (11803–6),[63] the basis of the forgiveness and of the hope is the message that "the exalted work" of "victory" over all the powers of evil, even "Satan, the old master," has now been accomplished, and with help that came "from the hands of the loving and holy women penitents" (11942–43), including the One Woman Penitent, Formerly Called Gretchen. As the drama turns out, then, "the young woman who is at first the object of Faust's purely sensual passion, inspired by Mephisto—Gretchen—becomes in fact Mephisto's victorious rival in the battle for Faust's soul."[64] For she is told that her elevation to "higher spheres" of glory will become the means for Faust to attain to it, too (12094–95).[65]

Those words are addressed to the Woman Penitent, Formerly Called Gretchen, by the Mater Gloriosa, seen as the special refuge for those who, like Gretchen, are "easy to seduce" and are "hard to

61. Jene Rosen aus den Händen / Liebend-heiliger Büßerinnen / Halfen uns den Sieg gewinnen, / Uns das hohe Werk vollenden, / Diesen Seelenschatz erbeuten. / Böse wichen, als wir streuten, / Teufel flohen, als wir trafen. / Statt gewohnter Höllenstrafen / Fühlten Liebesqual die Geister; / Selbst der alte Satansmeister / War von spitzer Pein durchdrungen. / Jauchzet auf! es ist gelungen.

62. Sündern vergeben, / Staub zu beleben.

63. Die sich verdammen, / Heile die Wahrheit; / Daß sie vom Bösen / Froh sich erlösen.

64. Buchwald 1964, 59.

65. Parallels in this to Walpurgis Night are itemized in Weyl 1971, 101–2.

save," but who are now "penitent women, in need of grace" (12013–25). The entire Chorus of Penitents addresses the Mater Gloriosa with the praise, "Thou dost soar to the heights of the everlasting kingdoms," and with the petition, "Receive our pleading, thou incomparable one, who art full of grace!" (12032–36).[66] She is "full of grace," as she had been addressed by the angel of the Annunciation, at any rate in the Latin of the Vulgate, "Ave, gratia plena, Dominus tecum."[67] The penitents are "in need of grace," and through her grace and purity their impurity is healed.[68] But the Mater Gloriosa does not represent the healing only of their individual lusts, nor only of Faust's conflicts; as has been said about such theological terms in this scene, "it is, of course, contrary to the sense to interpret them according to the strict sense of the terminology of the church, but it would be forcing things to exclude echoes of this completely."[69] Not only is it the case that "the several persons of Margarete-Galatea-Helen are now subsumed in the one person of Mary Mother of God";[70] but through these "echoes" of themes that have been sounding throughout the rest of the work, the several titles with which she is identified here in the closing scene may be said to resolve the conflicts between monotheism and both pantheism and polytheism, not by negating either of these but by exalting each to the level of the sublime, in "that loving fusion of pagan and Christian convictions in which Goethe as a new Hypsistarian found his own final religious peace."[71]

Those titles are brought together by Doctor Marianus, whose importance for the outcome of the drama has been well summa-

66. Du schwebst zu Höhen / Der ewigen Reiche, / Vernimm das Flehen, / Du Ohnegleiche, / Du Gnadenreiche!

67. Luke 1:28.

68. Emrich 1957, 418–19, has some warning observations on "grace" in *Faust.*

69. G. Müller 1933, 161n.

70. Atkins 1958, 172.

71. Jantz 1978, 48; according to the funeral oration of Gregory of Nazianzus for his father (*Orations* XVIII.5), the Hypsistarians rejected idols and sacrifices, but reverenced fire and lights, and "the Most High [Hypsistos]" was the only object of their worship—a heretical position with which Goethe, somewhat whimsically, identified himself.

rized in this sensitive observation: "As a sublime counter-figure to Doctor Faustus in his study at the outset of the drama, this mystical devotee of the Virgin represents the highest level of spiritual perfection attainable within the human sphere. Thematically he may be compared with Nereus in his devotion to Galatea in the final scene of the 'Classical Walpurgis Night.' Through Doctor Marianus the theme of the Eternal Feminine is re-introduced to *Faust* in its highest traditional form."[72]

Doctor Marianus brings the titles together in the final two lines of the worshipful ode with which he introduces the transcendent closing hymn. The ode is spoken first to the penitents: "Look upwards to this saving look, all who have been made tender through repentance, in order to transform yourselves thankfully into your blessed destiny."[73] Then Doctor Marianus turns to the Mater Gloriosa: "Let every higher sense be placed at thy service. *Virgin, Mother, Queen, Goddess:* continue to grant grace!" (12096–12103).[74] Such a heaping up of titles is a familiar device from earlier passages in the drama.[75] These four have been anticipated in the other ode of Doctor Marianus, shortly preceding this one: "The Glorious One in the center, in her wreath of stars, the Queen of Heaven. I can tell from her splendor. She is the Supreme sovereign of the World!" (11993–97).[76] And again: "Virgin, pure in the most beautiful sense, Mother worthy of honor, our chosen Queen, equal in birth to the gods" (12009–12).[77] He implores her to "grant approval to that which earnestly and tenderly moves this man's

72. Hamlin 1976, 304 n. 9. On the meaning of the title "Doctor Marianus," White 1980, 37–38.

73. Blicket auf zum Retterblick, / Alle reuig Zarten, / Euch zu seligem Geschick, / Dankend umzuarten.

74. Werde jeder beßre Sinn / Dir zum Dienst erbötig; / *Jungfrau, Mutter, Königin,* / *Göttin,* bleibe gnädig!

On the Mater Gloriosa and these titles, Möbus 1964, 291–95, urges that these lines not be read as Christian and Catholic.

75. For example, 1334, 9028–30, 9364.

76. Die Herrliche mitteninn / Im Sternenkranze, / Die Himmelskönigin, / Ich seh's am Glanze. / Höchste Herrscherin der Welt!

77. Jungfrau, rein im schönsten Sinn, / Mutter, Ehren würdig, / Uns erwählte Königin, / Göttern ebenbürtig.

breast and which with a holy passion of love he bears to thee" (12001–4).[78] He prays, "Let every higher sense be placed at thy service" (12100–12101).[79] By such petitions, the various yearnings and intuitions in "this man's breast," every "passion of love," including even Faust's original "coarse passion of love" (1114), and "every higher sense" of pantheism and polytheism as these have manifested themselves in Faust's development throughout the work are being raised to the exalted plane of the Virgin Mary, and thus of Christ her Son, and thus of God the Father in heaven (where this entire "postlude in heaven parallel to the 'Prologue in Heaven' "[80] is being played, with no action in heaven between these two scenes).

"In the soteriology, as in the ethics, of Goethe's play," one commentator has suggested, "love, not egoism, is both the principal instrument of Grace and the highest value."[81] The saving power of that love through each of the three occupants of that exalted plane—Mary, her Son Jesus Christ, and God the Father—has already been explicitly adumbrated by the Woman Penitent, Formerly Called Gretchen, while she is still alive on earth, in her penitential sighs for grace before the "devotional image of the Mater Dolorosa," as she prays a paraphrase of the medieval *Stabat Mater dolorosa:* "Incline thy countenance graciously to my need, thou who art abounding in pain. With the sword in thy heart and with a thousand pains thou dost look up at the death of thy Son. Thou dost look to the Father and send sighs upward for [thy Son's] trial and for thine own" (3588–95).[82] Now at the end, having become a participant in the grace and glory of heaven, she prays to Mary once more. Her prayer "is transposed into a radiant major key,"[83] and it is no longer addressed to the Mater Dolorosa but to

78. Billige, was des Mannes Brust / Ernst und zart beweget / Und mit heiliger Liebeslust / Dir entgegenträget.

79. Werde jeder beßre Sinn / Dir zum Dienst erbötig.

80. Jantz 1978, 101.

81. Dye 1977, 974.

82. Ach neige, / Du Schmerzenreiche, / Dein Antlitz gnädig meiner Not! / Das Schwert im Herzen [Luke 2:35], / Mit tausend Schmerzen / Blickst auf zu deines Sohnes Tod. / Zum Vater blickst du, / Und Seufzer schickst du / Hinauf um sein' und deine Not.

83. Fähnrich 1963, 257.

the Mater Gloriosa: "Incline, oh incline, thy countenance graciously to my happiness, thou incomparable one, thou radiant one!
The one whom I first loved, now no longer troubled, is coming
back" (12069–75).[84] The sharp contrast, and yet the special bond,
between Gretchen as the fallen woman, whom her own brother has
called "a whore" (3730), and Mary as the "Virgin, pure in the most
beautiful sense" (12009), becomes the subject of prayers to the
Virgin on Gretchen's behalf by the three Women Penitents of this
closing scene, with a devotional version of the logical argument *a
maiori ad minus.* "Thou who dost not deny thy presence to women
who have sinned greatly and dost elevate a repentant endeavor to
the level of eternity [which is how all three of them have been
treated, despite the magnitude of their sins], grant also to this good
soul, who forgot herself only once and who did not know that she
was doing wrong, thy fitting forgiveness!" (12061–68).[85] If even
they have not been denied the grace of forgiveness, she certainly
ought to receive it.

It is significant for this special bond that the prayer of each of
the three Penitents to Mary on behalf of Gretchen, and much
earlier Faust's lamentation over Gretchen, should contain the most
detailed references anywhere in the entire drama to the redemp-
tive work of Christ, who nevertheless "significantly, does not appear and is not invoked" directly as such even here.[86] When Mephistopheles sneers about Gretchen, "She is not the first,"[87] this is
apparently a verbatim quotation from the accounts of an actual
case that occurred in Frankfurt in 1771, as reported by Goethe.[88] It

84. Neige, neige, / Du Ohnegleiche, / Du Strahlenreiche, / Dein Antlitz
gnädig meinem Glück! / Der früh Geliebte, / Nicht mehr Getrübte, / Er
kommt zurück.

See the comments of Kommerell 1944, 125–26.

85. Die du großen Sünderinnen / Deine Nähe nicht verweigerst / Und ein
büßendes Gewinnen / In die Ewigkeiten steigerst, / Gönn auch dieser guten
Seele, / Die sich einmal nur vergessen, / Die nicht ahnte, daß sie fehle, / Dein
Verzeihen angemessen!

86. Emrich 1957, 418–419.

87. *Faust,* "Trüber Tag," 15 (Trunz 1968, 137); exactly the same already in
Urfaust (Trunz 1968, 415).

88. Hamlin 1976, 110 n. 2; Maier 1952, 125–47, discusses various attempts to
relate the tragedy of Gretchen to similar incidents that took place during Goethe's
lifetime.

may also echo Leporello's "nè la prima, nè l'ultima";[89] for according to Eckermann, Goethe once expressed the judgment that for an operatic setting of this drama, "the music would have to be in the manner of *Don Giovanni;* Mozart would have to compose the music for *Faust.*"[90] But Faust's reaction to the sneer is to explode, apparently in an allusion to the atoning death of Christ: "Not the first! How utterly miserable! No human soul can comprehend that more than one creature has descended to the depths of this misery, that the death-agony of the first was not enough to render satisfaction for the guilt of all the others in the eyes of the One who pardons eternally!"[91] Mephistopheles always has the typical devil's horror of the cross (10703–9), a horror that appears already in *Urfaust* (453–56), though Mephistopheles dismisses it as "a prejudice." In their original hostile encounter, Faust confronts Mephistopheles-as-poodle with the crucifix and with the death of Christ, whom he describes as "one without beginning, the ineffable one, who was poured out through all the heavens and was blasphemously pierced" on the cross (1298–1309).[92] And now, before Mary as Mater Gloriosa, each of the three penitents in her turn intones the litany, by referring to the person of Christ and citing the authority of some aspect of his life and death (12037–60).

The first is the Mulier Peccatrix of Luke 7:36–50. In the exegetical tradition, though not in the text of the Gospel, she was identified with Mary Magdalene, and is the Mary of whom the *Dies irae,* sung at the Requiem Mass for Gretchen's mother, prayed: "Thou who didst absolve Mary, and listen to the petition of the thief, thou hast also granted hope to me."[93] But it is striking that

89. Mozart, *Don Giovanni,* Act I, Scene 2.

90. Eckermann, *Gespräche mit Goethe,* Part Two, 12 February 1829 (Bergemann 1987, 293).

91. Die Erste nicht!—Jammer! Jammer! von keiner Menschenseele zu fassen, daß mehr als ein Geschöpf in die Tiefe dieses Elendes versank, daß nicht das erste genug tat für die Schuld aller übrigen in seiner windenden Todesnot vor den Augen des ewig Verzeihenden!

Faust, "Trüber Tag" (Trunz 1968, 137–138).

92. Kannst du ihn lesen? / Den nie Entsproßnen, / Unausgesprochnen, / Durch alle Himmel Gegoßnen, / Freventlich Durchstochnen?

93. Qui Mariam absolvisti / Et latronem exaudisti, / Mihi quoque spem dedisti.

this petition, with its confident reference to divine forgiveness, is omitted from the singing of the *Dies irae* in that scene in Part One (3798–3833), though it is echoed here in Part Two. Paraphrasing the Gospel text, the Magdalene bases her petition on Christ's statement that "her love proves that her many sins have been forgiven," and addresses it to the Virgin Mary: "By the love that made tears flow as balsam on the feet of thy divinely transfigured Son, despite the scorn of the Pharisees; by the jar that so richly poured out its incense; by the locks of hair that so gently dried the sacred limbs" (12037–44).[94] The second is the Mulier Samaritana, who, according to John 4:4–26, encountered Christ at the well.[95] She now makes "the well to which Abraham once brought his flocks to be watered" and at which "the cup was permitted to touch and cool the Savior's lips" into an allegory of the "superabundant, eternally clear fountain" of grace "that flows from there through all the worlds" (12045–52).[96] And the third is Maria Aegyptiaca, whose life is recorded not in the New Testament but in the *Acta Sanctorum*, including her conversion while on a pilgrimage to the Holy Sepulcher in Jerusalem, "the consecrated place where the Lord was laid to rest," and then her forty-seven years of penance as a hermit in the desert east of Jordan (12053–60).[97] Although it does seem "that according to the earliest conception of the closing scenes it was to be Christ who would free Faust's soul from hell after his victory over Lucifer,"[98] Christ himself does not appear directly and is not prayed to directly in these petitions; but in a prayer to Mary,

94. Bei der Liebe, die den Füßen / Deines gottverklärten Sohnes / Tränen ließ zum Balsam fließen, / Trotz des Pharisäerhohnes; / Beim Gefäße, das so reichlich / Tropfte Wohlgeruch hernieder, / Bei den Locken, die so weichlich / Trockneten die heil'gen Glieder.

95. Some notes on this in Mühlher 1957, 42–43.

96. Bei dem Bronn, zu dem schon weiland / Abram ließ die Herde führen, / Bei dem Eimer, der dem Heiland / Kühl die Lippe durft' berühren; / Bei der reinen, reichen Quelle, / Die nun dorther sich ergießet, / Überflüssig, ewig helle / Rings durch alle Welten fließet.

97. Bei dem hochgeweihten Orte, / Wo den Herrn man niederließ, / Bei dem Arm, der von der Pforte / Warnend mich zurücke stieß; / Bei der vierzigjährigen Buße, / Der ich treu in Wüsten blieb, / Bei dem seligen Scheidegruße, / Den im Sand ich niederschrieb.

98. Grumach 1952/1953, 76; also Arthur Henkel in Dürr and Molnár 1976, 288.

all of these references to the history of Christ are invoked in support of the petition for Gretchen—a reminiscence of the closing cantos of Dante's *Paradiso,* with the description of the Virgin Mary by Bernard of Clairvaux as "the one whose face most resembles that of Christ."[99]

But she is called "Virgin"—and then "Mother." This can be taken as an echo of the "pantheistic" reading of the Mothers in Part Two, for the theme of Nature as the All resounds here in the closing scene of *Faust.* Thus the content of redemption is defined as "being saved in the company of the All" (11807—8).[100] That "company of the All" is one of the very things which "earnestly and tenderly moves this man's breast and which with a holy passion of love he bears" to the Virgin Mother (12001—4).[101] In keeping with this "holy passion of love," the mighty forces of Nature, according to the Pater Profundus, "are messengers of love, they proclaim that which surrounds us in eternal creativity" (11882—83).[102] It does not seem to be an exaggeration to conclude that "this transfigured Nature becomes a metaphor of love. It is the only theme at the conclusion of Part Two of *Faust.*"[103] And just as those forces of a transfigured Nature surge everywhere and yet provide continuity and stability, "so it is almighty love that shapes and cares for the All" (11872—73),[104] apparently yet another echo of the *Paradiso,* this time of its closing line about "the love that moves the sun and all the other stars,"[105] as well as of the words of God to the angels in

99. "Riguarda omai nella faccia che a Cristo / più si somiglia, chè la sua chiarezza / sola ti può disporre a veder Cristo." Dante, *Paradiso,* Canto XXXII, lines 85—97. Pelikan 1990, 101—119.

The parallel to Dante may be intentional, as a way of speaking about Mary in the comprehensive title "Virgin" (12102). Schmidt 1901, 241—52, with a warning against excesses; but already Carus 1937, 80—82 (dated 5 April 1835), and, most recently, Luke 1990, 55—56.

100. . . . in dem Allverein / Selig zu sein.

101. . . . des Mannes Brust / Ernst und zart beweget / Und mit heiliger Liebeslust / Dir entgegenträget.

102. Sind Liebesboten, sie verkünden, / Was ewig schaffend uns umwallt.

103. Schlaffer 1981, 163.

104. So ist es die allmächtige Liebe, / Die alles bildet, alles hegt.

105. ". . . l'amor che move il sole e l'altre stelle." Dante, *Paradiso,* Canto XXXIII, line 145.

the Prologue in Heaven about being "embraced by that which is becoming, which works and lives eternally, with the chaste bonds of love" (346–47),[106] and of Faust's own reminiscence of his youthful sense of "the love of heaven" (771). Immediately preceding the prayer of the Pater Profundus, however, comes that of the Pater Ecstaticus, which opens by calling God "the eternal torch of joy, the glowing bond of love" (11854–55),[107] and closes with another reference to the theme of the All, but to a way of transcending it in eternal love, "until everything worthless is put to flight and what continues to shine is the star, the core of everlasting love" (11862–65).[108] That transcending even of the All in the Eternal is the fulfillment of the aspirations of Faust's scientific pantheism, for which "everything transitory is only a parable" of what abides (12104–5);[109] and it is this in Mary, not only as Virgin but as Mother (12102) and as the Eternal Feminine (12110).

Yet, in the words immediately preceding these, the Eternal Feminine who is Virgin and Mother is called "Queen" and "Goddess" as well (12102–3),[110] and is thus the fulfillment also of the aspirations of Faust's poetic polytheism, and specifically of the typology represented in the figures of Leda, Galatea, and above all Helen of Troy. Leda has appeared in a vision as "Queen" (6914), and Helen is repeatedly hailed simply with the title "Queen,"[111] even when she is being identified as the sacrificial victim.[112] Elsewhere it is as "the high Queen" that she is labeled (7294). Faust expands on the title, speaking to her as "the Queen" whose arrow had found its mark in him (9258–59)[113] and as "the Ruler who, the

106. Das Werdende, das ewig wirkt und lebt, / Umfass' euch mit der Liebe holden Schranken.

107. Ewiger Wonnebrand, / Glühendes Liebeband.

108. Daß ja das Nichtige / Alles verflüchtige, / Glänze der Dauerstern, / Ewiger Liebe Kern.

109. Alles Vergängliche / Ist nur ein Gleichnis.

110. It will be evident that I read the title "Göttin" for Mary differently from the way Thielicke 1982, 47, does.

111. 8592, 8640, 8904.

112. 8924, 8947, 8954.

113. Erstaunt, o Königin, seh' ich zugleich / Die sicher Treffende, hier den Getroffnen.

moment she appeared, assumed the throne" (9270–72).[114] She also uses the title "Queen" in referring to herself (8527, 8915). The title "Goddess," applied here at the end of the drama to Mary, is also used earlier for various deities: the Sun (1084); the Moon (7915, 8289); Nike (5450); Galatea (8147); and the Mothers (6213, 6218). Yet to Faust, Helen is the preeminent holder of that title, too. His incredulous exclamation at the initial vision of her, calling her "the sum total of the content of all the heavens," and asking, "Is it possible that something like this can be found on earth?" (2439–40),[115] already puts her into that realm.

But when she appears to him in person, coming back to life out of the mists of Classical antiquity, he tells her: "To you I owe the springs of every action and the quintessence of passion. I devote myself to you in affection, love, worship, yes in madness" (6498–6500).[116] The Poet, speaking for Faust and for all those present, proceeds to express that "worship" as, watching her kiss Faust for the first time, he describes her as "the Goddess" (6510). When she embraces Faust for the last time and disappears, leaving her garment behind, the Phorcyad tells him to keep the garment, because although "it is not the Goddess any more" and he has lost her, the garment is still "divine" (9948–50).[117] The vision of "godlike" feminine figures that Faust then experiences—followed immediately by a vision of "my most youthful summum bonum, of which I have been deprived for very long," which seems an obvious reference to Gretchen (10055–66)—may be seen as a precognition of the closing scene: "Yes, my eyes do not deceive me! I see it, on a sunlit couch, gloriously stretched out, but truly gigantic—the godlike form of a woman! It resembles Juno, Leda, Helen. With what

114. Zu deinen Füßen laß mich, frei und treu, / Dich Herrin anerkennen, die sogleich / Auftretend sich Besitz und Thron erwarb.

115. Den Inbegriff von allen Himmeln. . . . / So etwas findet sich auf Erden?

116. Du bist's, der ich die Regung aller Kraft, / Den Inbegriff der Leidenschaft, / Dir Neigung, Lieb', Anbetung, Wahnsinn zolle.

117. Halte fest! / Die Göttin ist's nicht mehr, die du verlorst, / Doch göttlich ist's.

majestic loveliness it shimmers before my eyes!" (10047−51).[118]
For to Faust, Helen is "the sole object of my yearning" (7412), but
she is more: "The eternal being, equal in birth to the gods, as great
as she is tender, as majestic as she is lovable!" (7440−41).[119] And
"equal in birth to the gods" is the very epithet used again here in
the closing scene by Doctor Marianus for Mary the Virgin (12012).
Under the titles Queen and Goddess, then, the Virgin is the sublime
monotheistic fulfillment of Faust's polytheistic vision of "the godlike form of a woman that resembles Juno, Leda, Helen," at the
beginning of Act IV of Part Two, just as she is, under the title
Mother, the monotheistic fulfillment of his pantheistic vision of
Nature as Mother at the beginning of Part One and elsewhere
throughout the drama and of his visit to the Mothers.[120] The title
addressed to her by Doctor Marianus, when "in mystical rapture"
he calls her "Supreme Sovereign of the World" (11997), likewise
seems to bring these two motifs together. In an ironic way, therefore, this fulfills eschatologically the prediction of Mephistopheles
after the potion in the Witch's Kitchen that Faust would now "see
Helen in every woman" (2603−4), except that what he now sees is
not Helen but Mary as he travels "from Gretchen and Helen
through Sophia, which brings with it the best of our inner life,
higher to Mary, who alone, as the supreme center of humanity, lifts
the upward look into the miracle of the mystery."[121]

The final salvation of Faust is assured when the angels, "leading away all that is immortal about Faust," snatch him from the
grasp of Mephistopheles (at 11824). And then, "bearing all that is
immortal about Faust," they proclaim it as an accomplished fact

118. Ja! das Auge trügt mich nicht!— / Auf sonnbeglänzten Pfühlen herrlich hingestreckt, / Zwar riesenhaft, ein göttergleiches Fraungebild, / Ich seh's!
Junonen ähnlich, Leda'n, Helenen, / Wie majestätisch lieblich mir's im Auge
schwankt.

There are thoughtful comments in Fairley 1953, 97−100; briefer comments in
J. Müller 1969, 217−18; and a note in Hamlin 1976, 256 nn. 1−2.

119. Das ewige Wesen, Göttern ebenbürtig, / So groß als zart, so hehr als
liebenswürdig.

120. Varying interpretations summarized by May 1962, 295−99.

121. Balthasar 1947, 514.

that "this noble member of the spirit world" has been "saved from evil," because someone "who always makes an effort in striving" can be redeemed. They add that the source of the salvation has been "participation of the love from above" (11934–41).[122] According to Goethe's own exegesis of these words as reported by Eckermann, "in these verses the key to Faust's salvation is contained: in Faust himself, an ever higher and purer activity until the end, and from above the eternal love that comes to his aid." Goethe added, in a defense (more or less accurate, depending on the specific identification of who and what may be meant by "*our* religious outlook") against the charge of Pelagian heresy: "This is completely in harmony with our religious outlook, according to which we are saved not merely through our own power but through the divine grace that is added to this."[123] Or, as he put it already in *Dichtung und Wahrheit,*

> What separated me from the *Unitas Fratrum,* as well as from other good Christian souls, was the very point on which the church has more than once fallen into dissension. On one hand, it was maintained that by the fall human nature had been so corrupted to its innermost core than not the least good could be found in it, and that therefore man must renounce all trust in his own powers and look to grace and its operations for everything. The other party, while it admitted the hereditary imperfections of man, nevertheless ascribed to nature a certain germ of good within, which, animated by divine grace, was capable of growing up to a joyous tree of spiritual happiness. By this latter conviction I was unconsciously penetrated to my inmost soul.[124]

Commentators on *Faust* have noted the parallels between the words about "growing up to a joyous tree" here and the language of God about the gardener and the tree in the Prologue in Heaven (310–11), as well as between the words "the hereditary imperfec-

122. Gerettet ist das edle Glied / Der Geisterwelt vom Bösen, / Wer immer strebend sich bemüht, / Den können wir erlösen. / Und hat an ihm die Liebe gar / Von oben teilgenommen, / Begegnet ihm die selige Schar / Mit herzlichem Willkommen.

123. Eckermann, *Gespräche mit Goethe,* Part Two, 6 June 1831 (Bergemann 1987, 471).

124. *Dichtung und Wahrheit,* 15.

tions of man" in this paragraph and in the song of the Chorus of Angels in the opening scene (740–41). Thus it is the "glowing bond of love" and "core of eternal love" proclaimed by the first of the Holy Anchorites, the Pater Ecstaticus (11854–65), and the "almighty love, which develops and preserves the All" (11866–89), praised by the second of the Holy Anchorites, the Pater Profundus, through which Faust is saved, by grace, but not without his own "striving." The ambiguity also in this closing scene, raises the question, however, "how far indeed the striving was necessary at all . . . since love is all-approving: we are perhaps confronted here with a paradox which will not answer to pressure."[125]

The third of the Holy Anchorites is the Pater Seraphicus, who connects this love to "the presence of God," to divine "revelation of eternal loving," and to "salvation," as he invites the Boy Souls to "rise upward to a higher circle and go on growing imperceptibly" (11918–25).[126] These opening words, "Rise upward," point in the same upward direction as the final words of the drama, "The Eternal Feminine leads us upward" (12110–11). The response of the Boy Souls to this invitation celebrates this salvation through the revelation of love as the vision of God: "Divinely instructed, you have the right to be confident that you will behold the One whom you worship" (11930–33).[127] This is clearly monotheistic, albeit in a highly idiosyncratic, even an ironic sense. To such a "monotheism" can be applied the words of Mephistopheles, that Faust serves God in a highly unusual way (300), as well as Margarete's comment that Faust's confession of faith is almost the same as what her own pastor says, albeit in different words (3459–61), both the confession of faith and the comment being "very seriously intended jests." Yet the Omega is like the Alpha. The words of the Lord God in heaven to the angels at the outset about the relation of the divine Reality to

125. Gray 1965–66, 374.
126. Steigt hinan zu höherm Kreise, / Wachset immer unvermerkt, / Wie nach ewig reiner Weise, / Gottes Gegenwart verstärkt. / Denn das ist der Geister Nahrung, / Die im freisten Äther waltet: / Ewigen Liebens Offenbarung, / Die zur Seligkeit entfaltet.
127. Göttlich belehret, / Dürft ihr vertrauen; / Den ihr verehret, / Werdet ihr schauen.

all other reality, urging them to "rejoice in the beauty that is living and rich" and to "make solid with your continuing thoughts that which floats in shifting appearances" (344–49),[128] also find their fulfillment when, back in heaven again, the Chorus Mysticus, invoking the apophatic language heard earlier (6222–24), celebrates the Ultimate Reality in its relation to that which floats in shifting appearances. For "everything transitory is only a parable. Here the inadequate becomes an event. Here the indescribable is accomplished. The Eternal Feminine leads us upward" (12104–11).[129]

128. Doch ihr, die echten Göttersöhne, / Erfreut euch der lebendig reichen Schöne! / Das Werdende, das ewig wirkt und lebt, / Umfass' euch mit der Liebe holden Schranken, / Und was in schwankender Erscheinung schwebt, / Befestiget mit dauernden Gedanken.

129. Alles Vergängliche / Ist nur ein Gleichnis; / Das Unzulängliche, / Hier wird's Ereignis; / Das Unbeschreibliche, / Hier ist's getan; / Das Ewig-Weibliche / Zieht uns hinan.

Bibliography

Amrine, Frederick, Francis J. Zucker, and Harvey Wheeler, eds. 1987. *Goethe and the Sciences: A Reappraisal.* Dordrecht: D. Reidel.

Arens, Hans. 1982. *Kommentar zu Goethes Faust I.* Heidelberg: Winter.

——. 1989. *Kommentar zu Goethes Faust II.* Heidelberg: Winter.

Aron, Willi. 1912–13. "Goethes Stellung zum Aberglauben." *Goethe-Jahrbuch* 33:42–66; 34:34–63.

Atkins, Stuart. 1952. "A Reconsideration of Some Unappreciated Aspects of the Prologue and Early Scenes in Goethe's *Faust.*" *Modern Language Review* 47:362–73.

——. 1953. "A Reconsideration of Some Misunderstood Passages in the Gretchen Tragedy." *Modern Language Review* 48:421–34.

——. 1954. "Goethe, Aristophanes and the Classical Walpurgisnight." *Comparative Literature* 6:64–78.

——. 1956. "Irony and Ambiguity in the Final Scene of Goethe's *Faust.*" In *On Romanticism and the Art of Translation: Studies in Honor of E. H. Zeydel,* 7–27. Edited by G. F. Merkel. Princeton: Princeton University Press for the University of Cincinnati.

——. 1958. *Goethe's Faust: A Literary Analysis.* Cambridge: Harvard University Press.

——. 1959. "Faustforschung und Faustdeutung seit 1945." *Euphorion* 53:422–40.

——. 1966. "Studies of Goethe's *Faust* since 1959." *German Quarterly* 39:303–10.

Balthasar, Hans Urs von. 1947. *Prometheus: Studien zur Geschichte des deutschen Idealismus.* 2d ed. Heidelberg: F. H. Kerle Verlag.

Bartscherer, Agnes. 1911. *Paracelsus, Paracelsisten und Goethes Faust.* Dortmund: F. W. Ruhfus.

Beddow, Michael. 1982. *The Fiction of Humanity: Studies in the Bildungsroman from Wieland to Thomas Mann.* Cambridge: Cambridge University Press.

Bennett, Benjamin. 1986. *Goethe's Theory of Poetry: "Faust" and the Regeneration of Language.* Ithaca: Cornell University Press.

Bergedorf, Max. 1881. *Faust und das christliche Volksbewusstsein.* Dresden: R. von Grumbkow.

Bergemann, Fritz, ed. 1987. Johann Peter Eckermann. *Gespräche mit Goethe in den letzten Jahren seines Lebens.* 3d ed. Baden-Baden: Insel Verlag.

Bergstraesser, Arnold. 1949. *Goethe's Image of Man and Society.* Chicago: Henry Regnery.

Beyschlag, Willibald. 1877. *Goethe's Faust in seinem Verhältnis zum Christenthum.* Berlin: L. Rauh.

Biese, Alfred. 1893. "Goethes dichterischer Pantheismus." *Berichte des freien deutschen Hochstifts,* n.s., 9:3–25.

Binswanger, Hans Christoph. 1985. *Geld und Magie: Deutung und Kritik der modernen Wirtschaft anhand von Goethes "Faust."* Stuttgart: Edition Weitbrecht.

Birven, Henri Clemens. 1924. *Goethes "Faust" und der Geist der Magie.* 2d ed. Leipzig: Talisverlag.

Bluhm, Heinz. 1966. "Die Entwicklung von Fausts erstem Monolog in der Szene 'Mitternacht' in Faust II, 5." *Forschen und Bilden: Mitteilungen aus den Nationalen Forschungs- und Gedenkstätten der klassischen deutschen Literatur in Weimar* (October 1966): 8–26.

Böhm, Wilhelm. 1933. *Faust der Nichtfaustische.* Halle: Max Niemeyer.

———. 1949. *Goethes Faust in neurer Deutung: Ein Kommentar für unsere Zeit.* Cologne: E. A. Seemann.

Boyd, James. 1932. *Goethe's Knowledge of English Literature.* Oxford: Clarendon Press.

Boyle, Nicholas. 1981. "Lessing, Biblical Criticism and the Origins of German Classical Culture." *German Life and Letters* 34:196–213.

———. 1987. *Goethe, "Faust," Part One.* Cambridge: Cambridge University Press.

———. 1991. *Goethe: The Poet and the Age.* 2 vols. projected. Oxford: Clarendon Press.

Brenn, Wolfgang. 1981. *Hermetik, geschichtliche Erfahrung, Allegorie: Die konstitutive Funktion von Goethes hermetisch beeinflußter Natur-*

philosophie für die allegorische Struktur des Faust II. Frankfurt: R. G. Fischer.

Bruford, Walter Horace. 1967. "Friedrich Theodor Vischer and His *Faust* Criticism." *Publications of the English Goethe Society,* n.s., 37:1–30.

Buchwald, Reinhard. 1964. *Führer durch Goethes Faustdichtung: Erklärung des Werkes und Geschichte seiner Entstehung.* 7th ed. Stuttgart: Alfred Kröner.

Burdach, Konrad. 1912. "Faust und Moses." *Sitzungsberichte der Preußischen Akademie der Wissenschaften, philosophisch-historische Klasse,* 358–403, 627–59, 736–89.

———. 1923. "Faust und die Sorge." *Deutsche Vierteljahrschrift für Literaturwissenschaft und Geistesgeschichte* 1:1–60.

———. 1926. "Die Disputationsszene und Grundidee in Goethes Faust." *Euphorion* 27:1–69.

———. 1932. "Das religiöse Problem in Goethes Faust." *Euphorion* 33:3–83.

Burger, Heinz-Otto. 1963. "Motiv, Konzeption, Idee—Das Kraftspiel in der Entwicklung von Goethes Faust." *Dasein heisst eine Rolle spielen: Studien zur deutschen Literaturgeschichte,* 144–93. Munich: Carl Hanser Verlag.

Burghold, Julius. 1913. "Die Faustwetten und ihre scheinbaren Widersprüche." *Goethe-Jahrbuch* 34:64–82.

Busch, Ernst. 1949. *Goethes Religion: Die Faust-Dichtung in christlicher Sicht.* Tübingen: Furche-Verlag.

Butler, Eliza Marian. 1948. *The Myth of the Magus.* Cambridge: Cambridge University Press.

———. 1952. *The Fortunes of Faust.* Cambridge: Cambridge University Press.

———. 1956. *Byron and Goethe: Analysis of a Passion.* London: Bowes and Bowes.

Capesius, Josef Franz. 1901. *Das Religiöse in Goethes Faust.* Hermannstadt: W. Krafft.

Carus, Carl Gustav. 1937. *Briefe über Goethes Faust.* Edited by Hans Kern. Hamburg: Kurt Saucke.

Cassirer, Ernst. 1963. *Rousseau, Kant and Goethe.* Translated by James Gutmann, Paul Oskar Kristeller, and John Herman Randall, Jr. Introduction by Peter Gay. New York: Harper Torchbooks.

Chiarloni, Anna. 1989. "Goethe und der Pietismus: Erinnerung und Verdrängung." *Goethe Jahrbuch* 106:133–59.

Cooledge, Charles Edwin. 1932. *The Religious Life of Goethe as Illustrated in the Tragedy of Faust.* Boston: Stratford.

Cornford, Francis MacDonald. 1957. *Plato's Cosmology: The "Timaeus" of*

Plato Translated with a Running Commentary. Reprint edition. New York: Liberal Arts Press.

Degen, Richard. 1906. *Der lutherische Charakter in Goethes "Faust."* Leipzig: Verlag für Literatur, Kunst und Musik.

Dieckmann, Liselotte. 1972. *Goethe's Faust: A Critical Reading.* Englewood Cliffs, N.J.: Prentice-Hall.

Diener, Gottfried. 1961. *Fausts Weg zu Helena: Urphänomenon und Archetypus.* Stuttgart: Ernst Klett Verlag.

Dietze, Walter. 1975. " 'Ich denke mir, der Teufel behalte unrecht': Bemerkungen zum Menschenbild in Goethes *Faust.*" *Publications of the English Goethe Society,* n.s., 45:1–22.

Dilthey, Wilhelm. 1964. *Weltanschauung und Analyse des Menschen seit Renaissance und Reformation.* 7th ed. Stuttgart: B. G. Teubner Verlagsgesellschaft.

Duck, Michael J. 1988. "Newton and Goethe on Colour: Physical and Physiological Considerations." *Annals of Science* 45:507–19.

Dürr, Volker, and Géza von Molnár, eds. 1976. *Versuche zu Goethe: Festschrift für Erich Heller.* Heidelberg: Lothar Stiehm Verlag.

Durrani, Osman. 1977. *Faust and the Bible: A Study of Goethe's Use of Scriptural Allusions and Christian Religious Motifs in Faust I and II.* Bern: Peter Lang.

Dye, Robert E. 1977. "The Easter Cantata and the Idea of Mediation in Goethe's *Faust.*" *PMLA* 92:963–76.

Dzialas, Ingrid. 1939. "Auffassung und Darstellung der Elemente bei Goethe." *Germanistische Studien* 216:141–63.

Eissler, Kurt Robert. 1963. *Goethe: A Psychoanalytic Study, 1775–1786.* 2 vols. Detroit: Wayne State University Press.

Emrich, Wilhelm. 1953. "Symbolinterpretation und Mythenforschung." *Euphorion* 47:38–67.

———. 1957. *Die Symbolik von Faust II.* 2d ed. Bonn: Athenäum-Verlag.

Enders, Carl Friedrich. 1948. *Faust-Studien: Muttermythos und Homunkulus-Allegorie in Goethes Faust.* Bonn: H. Bouvier.

Engard, Charles J. 1952. Introduction to Johann Wolfgang von Goethe, *Botanical Writings.* Honolulu: University of Hawaii Press.

Eppelsheimer, Rudolf. 1982. *Goethes Faust: Das Drama im Doppelreich.* Stuttgart: Verlag Freies Geistesleben.

Fähnrich, Hermann. 1963. "Goethes Musikanschauung in seiner Fausttragödie—Die Erfüllung und Vollendung seiner Opernreform." *Goethe: Neue Folge des Jahrbuchs der Goethe-Gesellschaft* 25:250–63.

Fairley, Barker. 1932. *Goethe as Revealed in His Poetry.* Toronto: University of Toronto Press.

———. 1936. "Goethe's Attitude to Science." *Bulletin of the John Rylands Library* 20:297–311.

———. 1947. *A Study of Goethe.* Oxford: Oxford University Press.

———. 1953. *Goethe's "Faust": Six Essays.* Oxford: Clarendon Press.

———. 1970. *Faust.* English translation, illustrated by Randy Jones. Toronto: University of Toronto Press.

Fiedler, Hermann Georg. 1946. *Textual Studies of Goethe's "Faust."* Oxford: Basil Blackwell.

Fischer, Kuno. 1878. *Goethes Faust: Über die Entstehung und Composition des Gedichts.* Stuttgart: J. G. Cotta.

Fischer, Kuno, ed. 1913. *Goethes Faust.* Edited by V. Michels. 4 vols. Heidelberg: C. Winter.

Fischer, Matthias-Johannes. 1983. *Rückgriff auf Goethe: Grundlagen einer kritischen Rezeptionsforschung.* Frankfurt: Peter Lang.

Floros, Constantin. 1977. *Die geistige Welt Gustav Mahlers in systematischer Darstellung.* Volume 1 of *Gustav Mahler.* Wiesbaden: Breitkopf und Härtel.

Frankenberger, Julius. 1926. *Walpurgis: Zur Kunstgestalt von Goethes Faust.* Leipzig: E. Wiegandt.

Frantz, Adolf Ingram. 1949. *Half a Hundred Thralls to Faust: A Study Based on the British and American Translations of Goethe's "Faust."* Chapel Hill: University of North Carolina Press.

Franz, Erich. 1932. *Goethe als religiöser Denker.* Tübingen: J. C. B. Mohr.

———. 1953. *Mensch und Dämon: Goethes Faust als menschliche Tragödie, ironische Weltschau und religiöses Mysterienspiel.* Tübingen: Max Niemeyer.

Frye, Northrop. 1986. *Northrop Frye on Shakespeare.* New Haven: Yale University Press.

Gantzer, C. J. Th. 1857. *Das Christliche in Goethe: Mit besonderer Berücksichtigung des "Faust."* Berlin: Vereins-Buchhandlung.

Gearey, John. 1981. *Goethe's "Faust": The Making of Part I.* New Haven: Yale University Press.

———. 1992. *Goethe's Other Faust: The Drama, Part II.* Toronto: University of Toronto Press.

Gillies, Alexander. 1957. *Goethe's Faust: An Interpretation.* Oxford: Basil Blackwell.

Girnus, Wilhelm. 1962. " 'Des Menschen Kraft, im Dichter offenbart': Dichter und Gesellschaft im Spiegel Goethes." *Goethe: Neue Folge des Jahrbuchs der Goethe-Gesellschaft* 24:1–32.

Goebel, Julius. 1909. "Goethes Quelle für die Erdgeistszene." *Journal of English and Germanic Philology* 7:1–17.

Görner, Rüdiger. 1989. "Vom Wort zur Tat in Goethes 'Faust'—

Paradigmenwechsel oder Metamorphose?" *Goethe Jahrbuch* 106:119–32.

Gräf, Hans Gerhard. 1904. *Goethe über seine Dichtungen.* 2. Theil, 2. Band. Frankfurt: Literarische Anstalt.

Gramsch, Alfred. 1949. *Goethes Faust: Einführung und Deutung.* Braunschweig: G. Westermann.

Gray, Ronald. 1952. *Goethe the Alchemist.* Cambridge: Cambridge University Press.

———. 1965–66. "Goethe's *Faust,* Part One"; "Goethe's *Faust,* Part Two." *Cambridge Quarterly* 1:125–43, 237–51, 355–79.

Greenberg, Martin, trans. 1992. Goethe. *Faust.* New Haven: Yale University Press.

Grumach, Ernst. 1952/1953. "Prolog und Epilog im Faustplan von 1797." *Goethe: Neue Folge des Jahrbuchs der Goethe-Gesellschaft* 14/15:63–107.

Guthke, Karl S. 1960. "Goethe, Milton und der humoristische Gott: Eine Studie zur poetischen Weltordnung im 'Faust.'" *Goethe: Neue Folge des Jahrbuchs der Goethe-Gesellschaft* 22:104–11.

Hagen, Benno von. 1940. "Fausts Hellasfahrt." *Goethe* 5:24–44.

Hahn, Karl-Heinz. 1979. "'Die Wissenschaft erhält ihren Werth, indem sie nützt': Über Goethe und die Anfänge der technisch-wissenschaftlichen Welt." *Goethe Jahrbuch* 96:243–57.

Hamlin, Cyrus, ed. 1976. Johann Wolfgang von Goethe. *Faust. A Tragedy: Backgrounds and Sources. Faust* translated by Walter Arndt. New York: W. W. Norton.

Hamm, Heinz. 1981. *Goethes "Faust": Werkgeschichte und Textanalyse.* 2d ed. Berlin: Volk und Wissen.

Harnack, Adolf. 1923. "Die Religion Goethes in der Epoche seiner Vollendung." *Erforschtes und Erlebtes,* 141–70. Gießen: A. Töpelmann.

Harnack, Otto. 1902. *Der Gang der Handlung in Goethes Faust.* Darmstadt: A. Bergsträsser.

Hartmann, Franz. 1900. *Betrachtungen über die Mystik in Goethes "Faust."* Leipzig: W. Friedrich.

Harvey, Paul. 1937. *The Oxford Companion to Classical Literature.* Oxford: Clarendon Press.

Hecker, Max, ed. 1907. Johann Wolfgang von Goethe. *Maximen und Reflexionen.* Weimar: Schriften der Goethe-Gesellschaft.

Heise, Wolfgang. 1976. "Der Entwicklungsgedanke als geschichtsphilosophische Programmatik: Zur Gemeinsamkeit von Herder und Goethe in der frühen Weimarer Zeit." *Goethe Jahrbuch* 93:116–38.

———. 1982. "Die Idee der Entwicklung im Spiegel von Goethes 'Faust

II' unter besonderer Berücksichtigung der Versuchungsdebatte, Vers 10128–10195." *Goethe Jahrbuch* 99:89–104.

Heisenberg, Werner. 1967. "Das Naturbild Goethes und die technisch-naturwissenschaftliche Welt." *Goethe: Neue Folge des Jahrbuchs der Goethe-Gesellschaft* 29:27–42.

Heller, Erich. 1952. *The Disinherited Mind: Essays in German Literature and Thought.* Cambridge: Bowes and Bowes.

———. 1966. *The Artist's Journey into the Interior.* London: Secker and Warburg.

Heller, Otto. 1931. *Faust and Faustus.* Saint Louis, Mo.: Washington University.

Henel, Heinrich. 1949. "Goethe und die Naturwissenschaft." *Journal of English and Germanic Philology* 48:507–32.

Henning, Hans, ed. 1970. *Faust-Bibliographie.* II. Teil, Band 2. Berlin and Weimar: Aufbau-Verlag.

Hering, Robert. 1952. *Wilhelm Meister und Faust und ihre Gestaltung im Zeichen der Gottesidee.* Frankfurt: G. Schulte-Bulmke.

Hertz, Gottfried Wilhelm. 1913. *Goethes Naturphilosophie im Faust: Ein Beitrag zur Erklärung der Dichtung.* Berlin: E. S. Mittler.

———. 1931. *Natur und Geist in Goethes Faust.* Frankfurt: M. Diesterweg.

———. 1932. "Zur Entstehungsgeschichte von Faust II, Akt 5." *Euphorion* 33:244–77.

Hippe, Robert. 1966. "Der 'Walpurgisnachtstraum' in Goethes 'Faust': Versuch einer Deutung." *Goethe: Neue Folge des Jahrbuchs der Goethe-Gesellschaft* 28:67–75.

Hoelzel, Alfred. 1988. *The Paradoxical Quest: A Study of Faustian Vicissitudes.* New York: Peter Lang.

Hof, Walter. 1939. "Fausts Ende." *Germanisch-Romanische Monatsschrift* 27:1–24.

Hoffmann, Reinhold. 1932–33. "Der Pantheismus in Goethes Werken." *Philosophie und Schule* 4:1–14.

———. 1955. "Die Entstehung des Faust-Manuskripts von 1825/26." *Euphorion* 49:283–304.

Hohlfeld, Alexander Rudolf. 1921. "Pact and Wager in Goethe's *Faust.*" *Modern Philology* 18:513–36.

———. 1936. "Zum irdischen Ausgang von Goethes Faustdichtung." *Goethe: Vierteljahrschrift der Goethe-Gesellschaft* 1:263–89.

Hohlfeld, Alexander Rudolf, Martin Joos, and William Freeman Twaddell, eds. 1940. *Wortindex zu Goethe's "Faust."* Madison: University of Wisconsin.

Holtzhauer, Helmut, and Bernhard Zeller, eds. 1968. *Studien zur Goethezeit: Festschrift für Lieselotte Blumenthal.* Weimar: Hermann Böhlaus Nachfolger.

Jaeger, Hans. 1949. "The Wald und Höhle Monologue in *Faust.*" *Monatshefte für den deutschen Unterricht* 41:395–402.

———. 1950. "The Problem of Faust's Salvation." *Goethe Bicentennial Studies* 109–52. Bloomington: Indiana University.

Jaeger, Werner. 1948. *Aristotle.* Translated by Richard Robinson. 2d ed. Oxford: Clarendon Press.

Jantz, Harold Stein. 1951. *Goethe's Faust as a Renaissance Man: Parallels and Prototypes.* Princeton: Princeton University Press.

———. 1952. "The Function of the 'Walpurgis Night's Dream.'" *Monatshefte* 44:359–408.

———. 1957. "The Symbolic Prototypes of Faust the Ruler." In *Wächter und Hüter: Festschrift für Hermann J. Weigand,* 77–91. Edited by Curt von Faber du Faur, Konstantin Reichardt, and Heinz Bluhm. New Haven: Yale University Press.

———. 1968. "Patterns and Structure in *Faust:* A Preliminary Inquiry." *Modern Language Notes* 83:359–87.

———. 1969. *The Mothers in Faust: The Myth of Time and Creativity.* Baltimore: Johns Hopkins University Press.

———. 1970. "The Mathematics of Faust's Rejuvenation." *Modern Language Notes* 85:383–85.

———. 1978. *The Form of Goethe's "Faust."* Baltimore: Johns Hopkins University Press.

Jarras, Félix. 1969. *La foi, les oeuvres et le salut dans le "Faust" de Goethe.* Paris: Lettres Modernes.

Jessen, Arnd. 1951. *Die zwölf Reiche der Seele nach Goethes Faust-Schema.* Berlin: Walter de Gruyter.

Jockers, Ernst. 1957. "Faust und die Natur"; "Im Anfang war die Tat?" *Mit Goethe: Gesammelte Aufsätze,* 90–147; 192–203. Heidelberg: Carl Winter Universitätsverlag.

Kalthoff, Albert. 1901. *Die religiösen Probleme in Goethes Faust.* Berlin: C. A. Schwetschke und Sohn.

Katz, Jay. 1972. *Experimentation with Human Beings.* New York: Russell Sage Foundation.

Kleinert, Paul. 1866. *Augustin und Goethe's Faust.* Berlin: Wiegandt und Grieben.

Klett, Ada Martha. 1939. *Der Streit um Faust II seit 1900: Chronologisch und nach Sachpunkten geordnet, mit kommentierter Bibliographie von 512 Titeln.* Jena: Frommann (W. Biedermann).

Kluge, Ingeborg. 1982. *Wissenschaftskritik in Goethes "Faust."* Frankfurt: Peter Lang.

Kohlschmidt, Werner. 1955. "Klassische Walpurgisnacht und Erlösungsmysterium: Zum Verhältnis von Antike und Christentum in 'Faust II.'" In *Form und Innerlichkeit: Beiträge zur Geschichte und Wirkung der deutschen Klassik und Romantik,* 97–119. Bern: Francke Verlag.

Kommerell, Max. 1944. *Geist und Buchstabe der Dichtung.* 3d ed. Frankfurt: Vittorio Klostermann.

Korff, Hermann August. 1938. *Faustischer Glaube: Versuch über das Problem humaner Lebenshaltung.* Leipzig: J. J. Weber.

———. 1966. *Geist der Goethezeit.* IV. Teil. 7th ed. Leipzig: Koehler und Amelang.

Köstlin, Karl Reinhold. 1860. *Göthe's Faust, seine Kritiker und Ausleger.* Tübingen: Laupp und Siebeck.

Kroner, Richard. 1957. "Goethe's Faust. The Tragedy of Titanism." In Nathan A. Scott, Jr., ed. *The Tragic Vision and the Christian Faith,* 153–73. New York.

Kühnemann, Eugen. 1938. *Goethes Faust und der Ostergedanke.* Breslau: Trewendt und Granier.

Kulp, Johannes. 1974. *Das Problem "Mensch" in Goethes Faust.* Wuppertal: H. Putty.

Landeck, Ulrich. 1981. *Der fünfte Akt von Goethes Faust II: Kommentierte kritische Ausgabe.* Zurich and Munich: Artemis Verlag.

Landsberger, Julius. 1882. *Das Buch Hiob und Goethes Faust.* Darmstadt: G. Jonghaus'sche Hofbuchhandlung.

Lange, Victor, and Hans-Gert Roloff, eds. 1971. *Dichtung, Sprache, Gesellschaft: Akten des IV. Internationalen Germanisten-Kongresses 1970 in Princeton.* Frankfurt: Beihefte zum Jahrbuch für Internationale Germanistik.

Lepinte, Christian. 1957. *Goethe et l'occultisme.* Paris: Publications de la faculté des lettres de l'Université de Strasbourg.

Levedahl, Kathryn S. 1970. "The Witches' One-Times-One: Sense or Nonsense?" *Modern Language Notes* 85:380–83.

Levinstein, Kurt. 1948. *Goethes Faust und die Vollendung des Menschen.* Berlin: Walter de Gruyter.

Loesche, Martin. 1944. *Grundbegriffe in Goethes Naturwissenschaft (und ihr Niederschlag im Faust).* Leipzig: E. A. Seemann.

Loewenich, Walther von. 1959. "Augustin und Goethe." In *Von Augustin zu Luther: Beiträge zur Kirchengeschichte,* 88–102. Witten: Luther Verlag.

Lohmeyer, Dorothea. 1975. *Faust und die Welt: Der zweite Teil der Dichtung.* 2d ed. Munich: C. H. Beck'sche Verlagsbuchhandlung.

Lohmeyer, Karl. 1927. "Das Meer und die Wolken in den beiden letzten Akten des Faust." *Jahrbuch der Goethe-Gesellschaft* 13:106–33.

Lukács, György. 1969. *Goethe and His Age.* Translated by Robert Anchor. New York: Grosset and Dunlap.

Luke, David. 1990. "'Vor deinem Jammerkreuz': Goethe's Attitude to Christian Belief." *Publications of the English Goethe Society,* n.s., 59:35–58.

Magnus, Rudolf. 1949. *Goethe as a Scientist.* Foreword by Günther Schmid. Translated by Heinz Norden. New York: Henry Schuman.

Mahal, Günther, ed. 1973. *Ansichten zu Faust: Karl Theens zum 70. Geburtstag.* Stuttgart: Kohlhammer.

Maier, Hans Albert. 1952. "Goethes Phantasiearbeit am Fauststoff im Jahre 1771." *PMLA* 67:125–46.

Mann, Thomas. 1968. "Über Goethe's Faust." *Schriften und Reden zur Literatur, Kunst und Philosophie,* 2:290–322. [1939.] Frankfurt: Fischer Bücherei.

Marotzki, Winfried. 1987. "Der Bildungsprozeß des Menschen in Hegels 'Phänomenologie des Geistes' und Goethes 'Faust.'" *Goethe Jahrbuch* 104:128–156.

Mason, Eudo Colecestra. 1959. "Some Conjectures regarding Goethe's 'Erdgeist.'" *The Era of Goethe: Essays Presented to J. Boyd,* 81–105. Oxford: Basil Blackwell.

———. 1960. "The Erdgeist Controversy Reconsidered." *Modern Language Review* 55:66–78.

———. 1962. "The Paths and Powers of Mephistopheles." *German Studies: Presented to Walter Horace Bruford,* 81–101. London: G. G. Harrap.

———. 1964. "Goethe's Sense of Evil." *Publications of the English Goethe Society,* n.s., 34:1–53.

———. 1967. *Goethe's "Faust": Its Genesis and Purport.* Berkeley: University of California Press.

Matthaei, Rupprecht. 1947. "Die Farbenlehre im 'Faust.'" *Goethe: Neue Folge des Jahrbuchs der Goethe-Gesellschaft* 10:59–148.

May, Kurt. 1962. *Faust II. Teil, in der Sprachform gedeutet.* Munich: Carl Hanser Verlag.

Meinhold, Peter. 1958. *Goethe zur Geschichte des Christentums.* Freiburg im Breisgau: Karl Alber.

Melzer, Friso. 1932. *Goethes "Faust": Eine evangelische Auslegung.* Berlin: Furche-Verlag.

Meyer, Herman. 1970. *Diese sehr ernsten Scherze: Eine Studie zu "Faust II."* Heidelberg: Stiehm.

Michelsen, Peter. 1962. "Fausts Erblindung." *Deutsche Vierteljahrschrift für Literaturwissenschaft und Geistesgeschichte* 36:26–35.

Mieth, Günter. 1980. "Fausts letzter Monolog—Poetische Struktur einer geschichtlichen Vision." *Goethe Jahrbuch* 97:90–102.

Möbus, Gerhard. 1964. *Die Christus-Frage in Goethes Leben und Werk.* Osnabrück: A. Fromm.

Mohr, Wolfgang. 1940. "Mephistopheles und Loki." *Deutsche Vierteljahrschrift für Literaturwissenschaft und Geistesgeschichte* 18:173–200.

Molnár, Géza von. 1981. "The Conditions of Faust's Wager and Its Resolution in the Light of Kantian Ethics." *Publications of the English Goethe Society,* n.s., 41:48–80.

Mommsen, Momme. 1953. "Zur Entstehung und Datierung einiger Faustszenen um 1800." *Euphorion* 47:295–330.

Morris, Max. 1902. "Swedenborg im Faust." *Goethe-Studien,* 13–41. 2d ed. Berlin: C. Skopnik.

Mühlher, Robert. 1957. "Der Lebensquell: Bildsymbole in Goethes Faust." *Deutsche Vierteljahrschrift* 31:38–69.

Müller, Adam. 1885. *Ethischer Charakter von Göthes Faust.* Regensburg: G. J. Manz.

Müller, Günther. 1933. "Die organische Seele im Faust." *Euphorion* 34:154–94.

Müller, Joachim. 1964. *Prolog und Epilog zu Goethes Faustdichtung.* Berlin: Akademie-Verlag.

———. 1969. *Neue Goethe-Studien.* Halle: Max Niemeyer Verlag.

———. 1972. *Zur Motivstruktur von Goethes Faust.* Berlin: Akademie-Verlag.

———. 1977. "Die tragische Aktion: Zum Geschehen im 5. Akt von 'Faust II' bis zum Tode Fausts." *Goethe Jahrbuch* 94:188–205.

———. 1980. *Die dramatische Funktion von Mephistos Monolog in Goethes "Faust" I: "Verachte nur Vernunft und Wissenschaft" (V. 1851–1867).* Berlin: Akademie-Verlag.

———. 1981. *Der vierte Akt im zweiten Teil von Goethes "Faust": Aktion und Bezüge.* Berlin: Akademie-Verlag.

Müllner, Ludwig. 1935. *Goethes Faust im Lichte seiner Naturforschung.* Basel: R. Goering.

Mulloy, William Joseph. 1944. *The German Catholic Estimate of Goethe (1790–1939): A Contribution to the Study of the Relation of German Catholicism to Secular Culture.* Berkeley: University of California Press.

Münzhuber, Joseph. 1947. *Das Religiöse in Goethes "Faust."* Nuremberg: Verlag Die Egge.

Nabholz, Johannes. 1956. "A Note on the Mothers in Goethe's *Faust.*" *Symposium* 15:198–203.

Nager, Franz. 1990. *Der heilkundige Dichter: Goethe und die Medizin.* Zurich: Artemis Verlag.

Naumann, Walter. 1952. "Goethe's Religion." *Journal of the History of Ideas* 13:188–99.

Neumann, Michael. 1985. *Das Ewig-Weibliche in Goethes "Faust."* Heidelberg: C. Winter.

Obenauer, Karl Justus. 1922. *Der faustische Mensch: Vierzehn Betrachtungen zum zweiten Teil von Goethes Faust.* Jena: Eugen Diederichs.

———. 1923. *Goethe in seinem Verhältnis zur Religion.* Jena: Eugen Diederichs.

Palmer, Philip Mason, and Robert Pattison More. 1965. *The Sources of the Faust Tradition: From Simon Magus to Lessing.* New York: Haskell House.

Parkes-Perret, Ford B. 1984. "Homunculus: Entstehungsrede und Ledatraumvision." *Goethe Jahrbuch* 101:244–49.

Pauly, August, Georg Wissowa, et al., eds. 1893–1963. *Real-Encyclopädie der klassischen Altertumswissenschaft.* Stuttgart: J. B. Metzler.

Pelikan, Jaroslav. 1971–89. *The Christian Tradition: A History of the Development of Doctrine.* 5 vols. Chicago: University of Chicago Press.

———. 1986. *Bach among the Theologians.* Philadelphia: Fortress Press.

———. 1990. *Eternal Feminines: Three Theological Allegories in Dante's "Paradiso."* New Brunswick, N.J.: Rutgers University Press.

———. 1993. *Christianity and Classical Culture: The Metamorphosis of Natural Theology in the Christian Encounter with Hellenism.* New Haven: Yale University Press.

Petsch, Robert. 1926a. "Die Geisterwelt in Goethes Faust." *Jahrbuch des freien deutschen Hochstifts* 1926:145–73.

———. 1926b. "Zur Chronologie des Faust." *Euphorion* 27:202–22.

Pfeiffer, Konrad. 1938. *Zum höchsten Dasein: Eine philosophische Fausterklärung.* Berlin: Walter de Gruyter.

Pinsk, Johannes. 1948. *Krisis des Faustischen: Unliterarische Betrachtungen zu Goethes "Faust."* Berlin: O. Arnold.

Poggioli, Renato. 1963. "Naboth's Vineyard, or the Pastoral View of the Social Order." *Journal of the History of Ideas* 24:3–24.

Powell, Jocelyn. 1970. "The Incarnation of Imagery in *Faust* Part I." *Publications of the English Goethe Society,* n.s., 40:95–116.

Raphael, Alice Pearl. 1965. *Goethe and the Philosophers' Stone: Symbolical*

Patterns in "The Parable" and the Second Part of "Faust." London: Routledge and Kegan Paul.

Rehder, Helmut. 1955. "The Classical Walpurgisnight." *Journal of English and Germanic Philology* 54:591–611.

Reimann, Hugo. 1967. *Christentum in Goethes "Faust."* Dornach: Kommission Philosophisch-Anthroposophischer Verlag am Goetheanum.

Reinhardt, Karl. 1960. "Die klassische Walpurgisnacht." In *Tradition und Geist: Gesammelte Essays zur Dichtung,* 309–56. Edited by Carl Becker. Göttingen: Vandenhoeck und Ruprecht.

Reiss, Hans Siegbert, ed. 1972. *Goethe und die Tradition.* Paperbound edition. Frankfurt: Athenäum Verlag.

Requadt, Paul. 1964. "Die Figur des Kaisers in Faust II." *Jahrbuch der deutschen Schillergesellschaft* 8:153–71.

———. 1972. *Goethes Faust I: Leitmotivik und Architektur.* Munich: Fink.

Resenhöfft, Wilhelm. 1973. "Faust, der Dreißigjährige." *Goethe Jahrbuch* 90:200–211.

Richter, Gottfried. 1973. *Faust: Ein christliches Mysterium.* Stuttgart: Urachhaus.

Rickert, Heinrich. 1930. "Der Erdgeist in Goethes Faust und die Erdgeisthypothese." *Jahrbuch des freien deutschen Hochstifts* 1930:91–130.

———. 1932. *Goethes Faust: Die dramatische Einheit der Dichtung.* Tübingen: J. C. B. Mohr (Paul Siebeck).

Rieger, Max. 1881. *Goethes Faust nach seinem religiösen Gehalte.* Heidelberg: C. Winter.

Riemann, Carl. 1962. "Goethes Gedanken über Kunst und Religion." *Goethe: Neue Folge des Jahrbuchs der Goethe-Gesellschaft* 24:109–34.

Rintelen, Fritz Joachim von. 1950. "Die Gottesidee bei Johann Wolfgang von Goethe." *Philosophische Jahrbücher* 60:7–19.

Rogge, Heinrich. 1921. *Symbol und Schicksal: Goethes Faust und seine Weisheit als Philosophie des Entwickelungsgedankens.* Prien am Chiemsee: Kampmann und Schnabel.

Roos, Carl. 1952. "Faust und die Zikade: Das Faustsymbol." *Euphorion* 46:31–47.

Rosenfeld, Hans-Friedrich. 1962. "Der Eingang des Johannesevangeliums im Mittelalter, mit einem Seitenblick auf Goethes Faust." In *Stoffe, Formen, Strukturen: Studien zur deutschen Literatur,* 178–205. Edited by Albert Fuchs and Helmut Motekat. Munich: M. Hueber.

Rowley, Brian A. 1983. "Steps to Heaven, and to the Abyss: Goethe's

Quantum Theory of Development." *Publications of the English Goethe Society,* n.s., 52:44–66.

Salm, Peter. 1971. *The Poem as Plant: A Biological View of Goethe's "Faust."* Cleveland: Press of Case Western Reserve University.

Salomon, Richard G. 1960. "The Grape Trick." In Stanley Diamond, ed., *Culture in History: Essays in Honor of Paul Radin,* 531–40. New York: Columbia University Press for Brandeis University.

Santayana, George. 1910. *Three Philosophical Poets: Lucretius, Dante and Goethe.* Cambridge: Harvard University Press.

Scheithauer, Lothar J., ed. 1959. Theodor Friedrich. *Kommentar zu Goethes Faust: Mit einem Faust-Wörterbuch und einer Faust-Bibliographie.* Stuttgart: P. Reclam.

Schiff, Julius. 1927. "Goethe und die Astrologie." *Preußische Jahrbücher* 210:86–96.

Schlaffer, Heinz. 1981. *Faust zweiter Teil: Die Allegorie des 19. Jahrhunderts.* Stuttgart: Metzler.

Schmid, Günther. 1940. *Goethe und die Naturwissenschaften: Eine Bibliographie.* Edited by Emil Abderhalden. Halle: Akademie der Naturforscher.

Schmidt, Erich. 1901. "Danteskes im Faust." *Herrigs Archiv für das Studium der neueren Sprachen und Literaturen* 107:241–52.

Schneider, Reinhold. 1946. *Fausts Rettung.* Berlin: Suhrkamp.

Schnitzer, Moriz. 1932. *Goethes Faust, eine Offenbarung über den Sinn des menschlichen Lebens als Gegenstück zum Evangelium.* Warnsdorf: Reformverlag.

Scholz, Heinrich. 1934. *Goethes Stellung zur Unsterblichkeitsfrage.* Tübingen: J. C. B. Mohr (Paul Siebeck).

Scholz, Rüdiger. 1982. *Die beschädigte Seele des grossen Mannes: Goethes "Faust" und die bürgerliche Gesellschaft.* Rheinfelden: Schäuble Verlag.

———. 1983. *Goethes "Faust" in der wissenschaftlichen Interpretation von Schelling und Hegel bis heute: Ein einführender Forschungsbericht.* Rheinfelden: Schäuble Verlag.

Schöne, Albrecht. 1982. *Götterzeichen—Liebeszauber—Satanskult: Neue Einblicke in alte Goethetexte.* Munich: Verlag C. H. Beck.

———. 1987. *Goethes Farbentheologie.* Munich: Verlag C. H. Beck.

Schott, Georg. 1940. *Goethes Faust in heutiger Schau.* Stuttgart: Tazzelwurm Verlag.

Schultz, Werner. 1928. "Zeit und Ewigkeit in der Weltanschauung Goethes." *Zeitschrift für Theologie und Kirche,* n.s., 9:288–309.

Schüpbach, Werner. 1980. *Die Menschwerdung als zentrales Phänomen der Evolution in Goethes Darstellung der Klassischen Walpurgisnacht.* 2d ed. Freiburg im Breisgau: Verlag Die Kommenden.

Schweitzer, Albert. 1961. *Goethe: Five Studies.* Translated by Charles R. Joy. Boston: Beacon Press.

Schwerte, Hans. 1962. *Faust und das Faustische: Ein Kapitel deutscher Ideologie.* Stuttgart: E. Klett.

Seeberg, Erich. 1932. "Goethes Stellung zur Religion." *Zeitschrift für Kirchengeschichte* 51:202–27.

Seidlin, Oskar. 1949. "Is the 'Prelude in the Theater' a Prelude to *Faust?*" *PMLA* 64:462–70.

Sepper, Dennis L. 1988. *Goethe contra Newton: Polemics and the Project for a New Science of Color.* New York: Cambridge University Press.

Shaffner, Randolph P. 1984. *The Apprenticeship Novel: A Study of the "Bildungsroman" as a Regulative Type in Western Literature with a Focus on Three Classic Representatives by Goethe, Maugham, and Mann.* New York: Peter Lang.

Sondrup, Steven P., and Randall L. Jones, eds. 1989. *Verskonkordanz zu Goethes "Faust, zweiter Teil."* Tübingen: Max Niemeyer.

Spengler, Oswald. 1983. *The Decline of the West.* Translated by Charles Francis Atkinson. 2 vols. New York: Alfred A. Knopf.

Spitta, Philip. 1951. *Johann Sebastian Bach.* Translated by Clara Bell and J. A. Fuller-Maitland. 3 vols. New York: Dover.

Spranger, Eduard. 1946. *Goethes Weltanschauung: Reden und Aufsätze.* Wiesbaden: Insel-Verlag.

Staiger, Emil. 1947/48. "Fausts Heilschlaf." *Hamburger Akademische Rundschau* 2:251–57.

Steinhauer, Harry. 1956. "Faust's Pact with the Devil." *PMLA* 71:180–200.

Steer, Alfred Gilbert. 1979. *Goethe's Science in the Structure of the Wanderjahre.* Athens: University of Georgia Press.

Streng, Georg. 1916. *Goethe's Faust als ein Versuch zur Lösung des Lebensproblems.* Munich: Müller und Fröhlich.

Strich, Fritz. 1949. "Homunculus." *Publications of the English Goethe Society,* n.s., 18:84–116.

Swales, Martin. 1978. *The German Bildungsroman from Wieland to Hesse.* Princeton: Princeton University Press.

Thielicke, Helmut. 1982. *Goethe und das Christentum.* Munich: R. Piper.

Thomas, Calvin, ed. 1892–97. *Goethe's Faust.* 2 vols. Boston: D. C. Heath.

Thomas, Keith. 1971. *Religion and the Decline of Magic: Studies in Popular Religion in Sixteenth- and Seventeenth-Century England.* London: Weidenfeld and Nicolson.

Thomte, Reidar. 1948. *Kierkegaard's Philosophy of Religion.* Princeton: Princeton University Press.

Trevelyan, Humphry. 1981. *Goethe and the Greeks.* Foreword by Hugh Lloyd-Jones. Cambridge: Cambridge University Press.

Trunz, Erich. 1968. *Goethes Faust kommentiert.* Hamburg: Christian Wegner Verlag.

Trunz, Erich, and Waltraud Loos, eds. 1971. *Goethe und der Kreis von Münster: Zeitgenössische Briefe und Aufzeichnungen.* Münster: Aschendorffsche Verlagsbuchhandlung.

Türck, Hermann. 1911. *Eine neue Faust-Erklärung.* 5th ed. Schwerin i. Mecklenburg: Stiller'sche Hofbuchhandlung.

————. 1917. *Faust—Hamlet—Christus.* Berlin: Wilhelm Borngräber.

————. 1921. *Goethe und sein Faust.* Leipzig: Wilhelm Borngräber.

Ugrinsky, Alexej, ed. 1987. *Goethe in the Twentieth Century.* Westport, Conn.: Greenwood Press.

Vogel, Hedwig. 1937. *Goethes Menschheitsidee in Naturschau und Dichtung dargestellt an Faust II.* Erlangen: Pall und Enke.

Vogel, Theodor, ed. 1943. *Gott, Gemüt und Welt: Goethes Selbstzeugnisse über seine Stellung zur Religion und zu religiös-kirchlichen Fragen.* [1888]. Edited by Rudolf Neuwinger. 3d ed. Leipzig: B. G. Teubner.

Walter, Bruno. 1958. *Gustav Mahler.* Translation supervised by Lotte Walter Lindt. London: Hamish Hamilton.

Wattenberg, Diedrich. 1969. "Goethe und die Sternenwelt." *Goethe: Neue Folge des Jahrbuchs der Goethe-Gesellschaft* 31:66–111.

Weber, Albrecht. 1958. *Wege zu Goethes "Faust."* Frankfurt: M. Diesterweg.

Wehnert, Bruno. 1908. "Gottvater, Erdgeist und Mephisto." *Zeitschrift für den deutschen Unterricht* 20:758–68.

Weisinger, Kenneth D. 1988. *The Classical Facade: A Nonclassical Reading of Goethe's Classicism.* University Park: Pennsylvania State University Press.

Weissleder, Karlernst W. 1936. *Goethes "Faust" und das Christentum.* Leipzig: S. Hirzel.

Wells, George A. 1965. "Goethe's Geological Studies." *Publications of the English Goethe Society,* n.s., 35:92–137.

Weyl, Shalom. 1971. "Ascent and Descent: Some Parallels between Faust's Salvation and the *Walpurgisnacht.*" *Publications of the English Goethe Society,* n.s., 41:91–102.

White, Ann. 1980. *Names and Nomenclature in Goethe's "Faust."* London: University of London Institute of Germanic Studies.

Wiemken, Helmut, ed. 1961. *Doctor Fausti Weheklag: Die Volksbücher von D. Johann Faust und Christoph Wagner.* Bremen: Carl Schünemann Verlag.

Wild, Gerhard. 1991. *Goethes Versöhnungsbilder: Eine geschichtsphiloso-*

phische Untersuchung zu Goethes späten Werken. Stuttgart: J. B. Metzlersche Verlagsbuchhandlung.

Wilkinson, Elizabeth Mary. 1972. "Goethe's *Faust:* Tragedy in the Diachronic Mode." *Publications of the English Goethe Society,* n.s., 42:116–74.

Wilkinson, Elizabeth Mary, ed. 1984. *Goethe Revisited: A Collection of Essays.* London: John Calder.

Wilkinson, Elizabeth Mary, and Leonard Ashley Willoughby. 1962. *Goethe, Poet and Thinker.* London: Edward Arnold Publishers.

Williams, John R. 1987. *Goethe's Faust.* London: Allen and Unwin.

Witte, William. 1959. "Goethe and ius naturale." In *Schiller and Burns and Other Essays,* 81–94. Oxford: Basil Blackwell.

Wittkowski, Wolfgang. 1968. " 'Gedenke zu Leben!' Schuld und Sorge in Goethes *Faust." Publications of the English Goethe Society,* n.s., 38:114–45.

Wittkowski, Wolfgang, ed. 1984. *Goethe im Kontext: Kunst und Humanität, Naturwissenschaft und Politik von der Aufklärung bis zur Restauration.* Tübingen: Max Niemeyer Verlag.

Wizenmann, Karl. 1932. *Faust und der Weg zum Leben: "Fausts Heimkehr."* 9th ed. Stuttgart: Wege-Verlag.

Wolff, Karl. 1949. *Fausts Erlösung.* Nuremberg: Nest-Verlag.

Wood, Henry. 1912. *Faust-Studien: Ein Beitrag zum Verständnis Goethes in seiner Dichtung.* Berlin: G. Reimer.

Wordsworth, Elizabeth. 1919. "Dante and Goethe." *Essays, Old and New,* 1–27. Oxford: Clarendon Press.

Würtenberg, Gustav. 1949. *Goethes Faust heute: Das Ende des faustischen Menschen.* Bonn: H. Hümmeler.

Zezschwitz, Eberhard von. 1985. *Komödienperspektive in Goethes "Faust I."* Bern: Peter Lang.

Ziolkowski, Theodore. 1972. *Fictional Transfigurations of Jesus.* Princeton: Princeton University Press.

———. 1989a. *German Romanticism and Its Institutions.* Princeton: Princeton University Press.

———. 1989b. *"Faust* and the University: Pedagogical Ruminations on a Subversive Classic." In *Texte, Motive, und Gestalten der Goethezeit: Festschrift für Hans Reiss,* 65–79. Edited by John L. Hibberd and H. B. Nisbet. Tübingen: Max Niemeyer Verlag.